The Truth Engine

The Truth Engine

Cross-Examination Outside the Box

Francis P. Karam

Illustrated by Jessica Hagy

Illustrations by Jessica Hagy

Cover design by Margaret Copeley

Layout by Matt Young

2nd printing June 2018, R. C. Brayshaw & Co., Lebanon, NH

ISBN 978-0-9990850-0-4

To Lisa, Nick, Ben, and Min
To my mother Alice, the very best nurse
And to my dad, Police Chief Frank Karam, who said,
"Son, just because it's legal doesn't make it moral."

About the Author

Francis (Frank) Karam began his education by studying the dead languages of Latin and Greek in high school, and then continued as a Classics major at Holy Cross College. Upon graduation, this background qualified him to work as a construction laborer, digging holes and operating a jackhammer, a task for which, his fellow hardhats informed him, he was not quite hefty enough. Therefore he enrolled in law school. Compared to reading about things like the Battle of Marathon and the murder of Agamemnon, he found law school pretty dry.

Frank began his legal career as a civil defense lawyer practicing admiralty law, another job for which he was not exactly suited. After that, he got a job as an assistant district attorney in the Bronx. Although the pay was lower than for construction work, it was a great job. Herman Melville wrote in Moby Dick, "A whale-ship was my Yale College and my Harvard." The Bronx was that for the author. There he learned that law is mostly not about law, but about facts and human nature. In the Bronx, he met and became lifelong friends with the street-smartest of lawyers, one of whom he married. He tried many cases, rising eventually to the Homicide Bureau.

After leaving the D.A.'s office, Frank practiced criminal defense, a job that is not mainly about defense, but attacking the prosecution's case using cross-examination. In this practice he spent more than a decade learning, watching, and doing cross-examination. After that he became a securities-fraud class-action plaintiff's lawyer, another job that involves building a case through the questioning of hostile and evasive witnesses. He continues in that work at present.

Throughout his career as a cross-examiner, Frank learned that if you take the obvious path, you won't be able to compete with big corporations, the government, and other powerful, smart adversaries. That's how he came to draw on the history of ancient battles and dramas and the thinking of scientists, financiers, psychologists, and military strategists for ideas, tactics, and strategies for trials and cross-examination. If you're interested in his formal CV it can be found at https:// www.rgrdlaw.com/attorneys-Francis-P-Karam.html.

About the Illustrator

Seattle illustrator and writer Jessica Hagy is well known for capturing essential wisdom in simple, witty graphs, pie charts, and Venn diagrams on 3 x 5 cards. Her work has appeared in the *New York Times, Forbes, US News & World Report*, and many other publications and media outlets. She is the author of six books, including *The Art of War Visualized, How to Be Interesting,* and *Indexed.* She was the winner of *Time Magazine*'s Best Blogs of 2008 and the *Guardian*'s Best of the Internet award, among numerous other awards.

[Cross-examination] is beyond any doubt the greatest legal engine ever invented for the discovery of truth. . . . Cross-examination, not trial by jury, is the great and permanent contribution of the Anglo-American system of law to improved methods of trial-procedure.

—John Henry Wigmore, *A Treatise on the System of Evidence in Trials at Common Law* (1904–05)

Contents

10 Questions for Cross-Examiners

As you prepare and present your next case, I invite you to ask yourself the following questions, taken from the ten chapters of the book. They all pertain to the main purpose of cross-examination: getting to the truth.

1. What truth is beneath the surface at the heart of the matter?

2. Have I broken my case down into its smallest parts?

3. Am I missing the most important thing, one of the Big Facts at the center of the case?

4. Have I immersed myself deeply in the case so that I understand it from all angles, including my adversary's position?

5. What can I leave out of this case to make it easier for the judge and jury to see the truth?

6. What is the real story of this case? What is the deep conflict? Where are the beginning, the middle, and the end of the story?

7. How can I "tell all the truth but tell it slant," as poet Emily Dickinson says? How can I use stealth to get a reluctant witness to reveal the truth?

8. What strategy is the witness using to evade the truth? What is the right tool to deal with it?

9. Am I thinking with my whole body, not just my head?

10. What basic principle can I return to in this case to find an answer, solve a problem, or create a solution? What can I learn from other competitive disciplines?

Preface

FROM THE FIRST TIME I did a cross-examination, I have been fascinated by it. Some think of cross-examination as an arcane dark art that tricky lawyers practice. But I have found it to be a very human method of thinking, connected to the deep natural ways that humans find things out and communicate with one another. Isn't asking questions to find out the truth a good way to survive and succeed in life?

Although not dark and tricky, cross-examination is intuitive and somewhat mysterious. Some questions led me to write this book. What goes on in the mind of a cross-examiner? How does your brain work when you're cross-examining? How does that great question pop out in the heat of an exchange? What can you do to make that intuitive flash happen?

Cross-examination is an underestimated thinking tool. It is much deeper and more powerful than is appreciated. Think about how important trials—criminal or civil cases that have a large impact on individuals and on society—can be decided by cross-examination. But only a handful of books have been written on the subject. Contrast this with the number of books written about chess, another face-to-face contest that employs intelligence and strategy. There are thousands of books about chess. Yet how many lives have depended on a chess game? How many big corporations have risked billions of dollars on the outcome of a chess game? Cross-examination is far more important, but it has not received the attention that it deserves.

If cross-examination really is, as Wigmore said, an engine for the discovery of truth, then—keeping with the metaphor—the mechanics of it must be important. Important not only for law, but for other areas of life where truth matters. And if that is so, then those other areas of life could provide insight into cross-examination.

This book is different from other books on cross-examination. I wanted to go deeper than simply rules, tips, or maxims. I try to look into cross-examination as a form of perceptual, factual, physical reasoning (that is, thinking with the whole body, not just the head), and to look at questions as the most powerful thinking tools.

This is not to say that I haven't read and benefited from other books on cross-examination that offer tips and maxims. I encourage any reader of this book to read those also. In particular I like John Nicholas Iannuzzi's *Handbook of Cross Examination: The Mosaic Art*, Irving Younger's Ten Commandments of Cross-Examination in *The Art of Cross-Examination*, James McElhaney's chapters on cross-examination in *McElhaney's Litigation*, and Peter Megargee Brown's *The Art of Questioning: Thirty Maxims of Cross-Examination*. I recently reread Francis Wellman's *The Art of Cross-Examination* and found it far more valuable than when I read it as a younger lawyer.

In fact I wish there were more books published on cross-examination. One of the things that I discovered while writing this book is that no one book can exhaust the subject. There are other topics I could have included in this one but had to leave out if I was ever to finish. I hope that those who disagree with or wish to expand on the ideas in this book will make their own contributions to the literature.

An important purpose of this book is to try to understand the how and why behind the maxims and tips that are taught to cross-examiners. I hope that this book will be more a "how to be a cook" book than a book of recipes, and a look at what lies below the water rather than just the tip of the iceberg. In particular, I want to explore the process of human thinking that creates good cross-examination.

I hope that young lawyers who read this book will be better able to understand and use Younger's Ten Commandments of Cross-Examination and Megargee Brown's maxims. I hope that more experienced lawyers will take the ideas here and use them creatively to make even more brilliant cross-examinations.

Since this book tries to understand cross-examination as connected to other kinds of human thinking, I stray quite far from the law and legal books. In my thirty-five years of lawyering, I have found that walking off the beaten path has helped me to meet the creative challenges of each new cross-examination. If you're always within the four corners of the law, the case, the facts, and the documents you're given, you may never find that creative insight. This is why in this book there is more discussion about science, finance, storytelling, strategy, physical action, and psychology than about law and the rules of evidence. These topics reflect my eclectic journey from courtroom experiences (and failures) to questions, seeking answers, looking for and reading nonlaw books that described what I experienced, as well as observations gained from teaching with the National Institute of Trial Advocacy.

Each turn, from doing, to reading, to teaching, and then back to doing, gave me a better understanding. What I have discovered is that cross-examination is not isolated or arcane, but a valuable liberal art worthy in itself of study and exploration. It is also a practical and useful art, not only in trials but in all areas of law and beyond that in other areas of life. In fact there are many books, anchors, and activities that have nothing to do with law that can be studied and enjoyed and then brought back to make better cross-examinations. Cross-examiners can learn as much from Aristotle, Bruce Lee, or physicist Richard Feynman as from Irving Younger.

One of the most interesting things about cross-examination is that even though there are commandments, rules, and maxims, sometimes the best questions break those. Sometimes the best questions are not only counter-intuitive, but counter to what I thought was logical. I always have the feeling that there is somewhere deeper to go and that the truth somehow lies at the bottom of it all. If you ask a question that reveals the truth, the rules don't matter. There is a lot of unexplored territory for those inclined to take risks and explore, and there will be joy in finding things out. Cross-examination that reveals the truth serves an important role in our society. Lawyers who seek out and reveal the truth are useful to their clients and to the law itself, and more valuable than those who have narrower or more self-serving goals.

Cross-examination demands a high level of performance, creativity, and competitiveness. I hope this book will help each reader meet that challenge in ways you have perhaps not considered before.

Acknowledgments

I WOULD LIKE TO EXPRESS MY THANKS to all those lawyers whose cross-examination I watched and learned from, including my friends from the Bronx D.A.'s office. Also thanks to NITA (the National Institute of Trial Advocacy), to my fellow teachers, and to my students, from whom I am always learning. Thanks to Assistant Dean Andrew Rossner of Rutgers Law School, from whom I borrowed (or stole with permission) the cross-examination example in chapter 2. Also thanks to Susan Kaplan and Ellen Neuborne for their early editing work and to Jessica Hagy for her brilliant illustrations. Finally, thanks to my editor, Margaret Copeley, to whom I brought a chaotic bucket of ideas and who helped me make it into this book.

Part 1

TRUTH

CHAPTER 1

TRUTH AND UNCERTAINTY

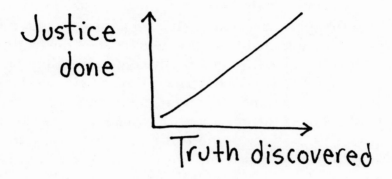

It had the added advantage of being true.

—Henry Kissinger

TRUTH IS THE ULTIMATE GOAL of our legal system. The advocacy system is based on the theory that if each side diligently represents its client, and no one outright lies, the truth will prevail and justice will get done.

Unfortunately the real world is not so neat and certain. Still, there is usually a fact, a truth at the center of each case. And like the sun in the center of the solar system, the force of this truth pulls and influences the evidence, facts, events, and witnesses in the case. The influence is sometimes open and clear, but often not and you have to dig and think and analyze to get to it. Getting to this truth, understanding it, and basing your case on it is the essence of trial strategy and cross-examination.

The title of this book, referring to cross-examination as a truth engine, comes from the famous quote in the opening epigraph from John Henry Wigmore (1863–1943), an expert in the law of evidence. The quote is the seed that got me thinking about the idea of truth in cross-examination and trial. If you don't seek the truth, how can you do what Wigmore says cross-examination is meant to do—discover the truth? If we're always trying to win, and making the best argument and presenting the best facts for our client, how can a lawyer ask the questions that get to the truth? If your case is not seeking truth and based on truth, then how can you best operate the machinery of the truth engine?

When I started my career, I bought into many of the things I was told in law school. "You can't really know the truth, you can only look at the evidence." "You're not a witness, you're a lawyer." "The truth is a tricky thing." The message was to be wary of the truth and trust in process, argument, analysis, evidence, and advocacy. But I always found that the truth was under there somewhere, like the hidden foundation of a building, supporting all the rest—the perceptions, arguments, and narratives, both true and false.

I found that digging for this foundation was the best way to approach trial work and cross-examination. Focusing on process, analysis, and argument can distract from the truth. In the dynamic, give-and-take world of trials and cross-examination, searching for the truth at all times and at every stage is the best way to work.

I have heard many stories of lawyers who first went desperately looking for a book on how to cross-examine just before they had to question a witness at a trial, hearing, or deposition. That last-minute panic is why Irving Younger's Ten Commandments of Cross Examination,[1] written forty years ago, are so compelling: you can read them in a few minutes and put them into practice. Younger (1932–1988), Assistant U.S. Attorney, judge, and law professor, offered the following succinct principles:

1. Be brief.

2. Use plain words.

3. Use only leading questions.

4. Be prepared.

5. Listen.

6. Do not quarrel.

7. Avoid repetition.

8. Disallow witness explanation.

9. Limit questioning.

10. Save for summation.[2]

Since Wigmore pointed out that the purpose of cross-examination is to discover the truth, it is remarkable that Younger makes no mention at all of the truth in his Ten Commandments. Although his rules are very useful for cross-examiners, they don't really satisfy Wigmore's simple definition of cross-examination as a truth engine. I consider Younger's rules the tip, or at

---

[1] Irving Younger, *The Art of Cross-Examination* (Chicago: American Bar Association, 1976).

[2] Thomas W. Cranmer and David D. O'Brien, "The Art of Cross-Examination," *Michigan Bar Journal*, August 2013: 54–56.

least one tip, of the huge iceberg of knowledge, thinking, and strategies of cross-examination. Lawyers and others who want to become better thinkers should be aware of and study this body of knowledge over time, throughout any career that requires intelligent speaking and thinking.

Law school consists mostly of reading appellate opinions that begin by stating the law and then applying what the judge represents as a static, established set of facts. Lawyers are trained to marshal the facts. There are few, if any, courses on investigating or finding facts and interviewing witnesses. In law school, the facts are just there on the page. But in the real world, understanding what appear to be facts in order to find the truth is an ongoing full-time job.

What Is Cross-Examination?

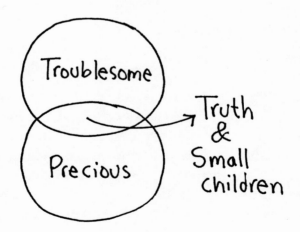

For my first heresy in this book I present my definition of cross-examination: *Cross-examination is asking questions that reveal the truth.*

What's heretical about that? Lawyers are not really supposed to care about the truth as their first priority. They're supposed to be zealous advocates on behalf of their clients. In my experience, often someone who is zealous about something cares little for the truth.

My definition of cross-examination says nothing about winning trials, the rules of evidence, or the exclusivity of the dark art of cross-examination to those most brilliant members of the bar. According to my definition, you don't even have to be a lawyer to cross-examine. You only need to ask questions that reveal the truth.

The catch is that in order to ask questions in cross-examination that *reveal* the truth, you must first ask questions to *find* the truth both before and during trial. That is an important part of this book.

What Is Truth and How Do We Find It?

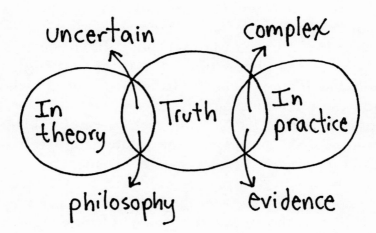

I'm sure that entire philosophical books have been written about what truth is. We are dealing with the real world and legal cases here, so we can define truth in more practical terms. To start with, the truth is what really happened. It is what the evidence reveals as certainty—if enough evidence can be found and it is evaluated objectively without bias or thinking errors.

This fact about the truth is often overlooked by lawyers: the truth is not a single fixed entity. It includes everything that relates to the case, not just the facts of the case. It evolves over the course of a case and changes in different contexts and perspectives, especially during the trial. Therefore the truth also is what is actually happening at any given time from the start of the case to the end. It is the slant that your client puts on the case when you first meet. It is the evasion of a witness you interview. It is the determination of the detective on the case, or the aloof arrogance of the CEO of the company you represent. It is the judge's ideological leanings, or the expression on her face when a witness at trial changes the judge's previous view of the case. None of these examples are part of the "facts of the case" that you learn in law school, but all are important parts of the truth of the case.

Hard evidence—photographs, video or audio recordings, cell phone location data, or written documents like e-mails—may be true but is not the whole truth. Data like these are the foundation of the truth, but not the truth itself. From each piece of evidence, you must make an inference or a statement describing the data, and already, even with a statement as simple as a description of a photograph, you're in danger of error and of straying from the truth. The more abstract the evidence, the more risk there is of losing the truth. Yet you must build further on this uncertain foundation of data and make inferences to make more complex statements, like timelines, maps, and descriptions of events, that are part of the whole story.

Finally, you must process and organize those building blocks into a narrative or story that you want to represent as the truth at the highest level. This process has been compared to a puzzle or a mosaic.[3] Another way to view it is to picture a tree, with the data as the trunk and the statements and inferences as the larger branches, or a river with small streams flowing into it. The more inferring, thinking, and processing you do, the farther out on the branches you climb and the more dangerous your climb becomes. Rather than continuing to go farther out on these limbs, you need to continually return to searching for the truth that is at the center of the case.

Truth and Cross-Examination Strategy

I have still not said anything about winning arguments or trials. I believe that if you seek the truth—if

---

[3] See for example John Nicholas Iannuzzi, *Handbook of Cross Examination: The Mosaic Art*, 3rd edition (Bloomington, IN: Xlibris, 2011).

you approach the facts and the evidence with a strong sense of curiosity, perception, and critical thinking— you will find it, or at least get as close as possible to it. If you follow the principles in this book you will learn how to reveal the truth even when the person you're questioning resists the truth. If you're coming from a base of the truth, you will be a better person and a better lawyer, and you will win a lot more trials and arguments than you will lose. In the long term you will have a successful career based in integrity.

The epigraph to this chapter is an ironic statement by Henry Kissinger, and I use it ironically to introduce a chapter that advocates seeking the truth. Kissinger was and still is a brilliant practitioner of realpolitik in the tradition of Machiavelli. His statement, "It had the added advantage of being true," is a coy and witty acknowledgment that he usually didn't care if the points and arguments he made were truthful, but if he had the truth on his side, all things being equal, he would have more weight and advantage. Falsehood and deception are much more likely to be caught out in a courtroom setting than in international politics. In most cases that go to trial, all things are in fact very close to equal. Why not find and seek the truth for the "added advantage"?

In the great majority of cases, at some point—usually very late in the case—the truth becomes clear. Somehow it all comes together, but often too late for the lawyer on the wrong side to realize it and act on it. The lawyer who finds the truth at the earliest possible time and bases case strategy, decisions, and cross-examination on the truth will occupy the high ground in the contest of trial. Trying to figure out the truth early on will give you the edge to win more trials because you will be the reality-based lawyer while your opponent is most likely theory based, and also because our jury-trial system, despite all of its flaws and uncertainties, more often than not gives a result based on the truth. Why not put that percentage in your favor, even if it's not 100 percent?

The Right Question at the Right Time

Seeing the truth is a significant advantage for decision making under pressure. A trial is fast moving by necessity (compared to everything else in our glacially paced discipline of law), and cross-examination is the fastest-moving phase of a trial. It is hard to see and understand what is going on in any fast-moving activity. There are levels of reality that are hard to see beyond whatever is most salient. It is often difficult to figure out just what is going on in the courtroom until afterward when you have had time to reflect. But every outcome—such as a verdict in your client's favor—must come from a set of present facts or conditions, some known and some not. The better you can perceive the truth that is unfolding in the present, both obvious and subtle, the more you are able to influence the outcome.

But what if the truth goes against your side? In that case it's better to have the knowledge that will allow you to settle or reach a plea deal rather than going to trial when a loss seems likely. Seeing the truth is especially important in cases where the truth is hard to determine. Those are the cases that go to trial, and in these close cases, getting to the truth will make you the better lawyer and a better performer at trial. It will help you realize at the earliest possible time if the truth is not on your side and help you make the best decision for your case and your client.

Understanding when you know the truth and when you do not is a key advantage at each point in a case and a trial. In criminal defense cases where you must go to trial there may be a gap between the truth and the evidence. That is, the truth of whether the accused committed the crime cannot be known for sure (because most clients in criminal cases that go to trial deny their guilt even to their own lawyer), but the truth of a number of facts is known. In that case, seeing these facts truthfully, without bias or rhetoric, and letting the facts tell the truth is your best strategy. In this example the truth may be closer to "the evidence does not prove guilt" than to "my client didn't do it."

You might be thinking, "Isn't this obvious? Isn't this what every lawyer does — evaluate whether the evidence can prove a case?" I have been surprised at how many smart lawyers have failed to see the truth when it was right in front of their eyes or have been misled by non-truths and lost cases. The simple awareness that seeing the truth and avoiding deception — including self-deception — is a skill that needs to be constantly practiced will win you many trials that you would otherwise lose.

Legal concepts of admissibility, relevance, and weight are the law's apparatus for the truth-finding process. In any trial, you will have to make dozens, sometimes hundreds of decisions about objections, arguments, questions, and evidence. If you're coming from the direction of the truth rather than what helps you win, your judgment will be better and you will make better decisions in the many small steps that go into a successful trial.

Often winning a case depends on avoiding errors, misjudgments, and biases, and that depends on perceiving and using the truth. Sticking to the truth may not win every trial, but it will allow you to avoid major blunders. Before you make an argument or ask a cross-examination question, ask yourself as a final check, "Is this really the truth?" You will then be more careful with facts, which are dear to the hearts of judges everywhere.

You will make mistakes at trial and mistakes in judgment, but if you remain focused on the truth your mistakes will be less harmful. They will be mistakes that you can recognize and accept on the way to the right answer, rather than wasted detours into strategies and arguments that blow up or prove useless. Every small loss, every mistake can become part of your larger view of the case, which you will arrive at sooner than a lawyer who is not looking for the overall truth.

Why Lawyers Overlook the Truth

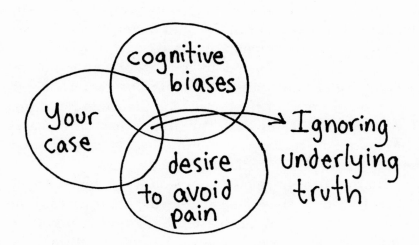

The truth lurks like a shadow elephant on the periphery of our vision because we never really focus on it or go after it, even though we know it's out there somewhere. Most lawyers do not, as their first goal, seek the truth. Why is that, if truth is the ultimate goal of our legal system? There are many complex factors within all the parties involved—lawyers, judges, juries, litigants, and witnesses—and in the legal system that undermine getting to the truth. For the moment let's examine the factors within lawyers themselves. These have to do largely with how the human mind and emotions work. Understanding these factors and working with them is key to winning cases.

The truth is like six-pack abs. They're a great thing, and intellectually everyone knows what you have to do to get them—just do 500 sit-ups a day and eat 500 fewer calories a day—but very few people have ripped abs because that kind of day-to-day behavior is hard to sustain. *The human brain has a tendency to lapse into the easiest available behavior.* This is just as true for thinking as for exercise and eating, and so just as most lawyers come up short of a six-pack physically, we also slip from the consistent discipline and focus we need to see the truth as it develops in our cases.

After getting burned by the theory-first method when I failed to recognize the truth or new facts about my cases, I decided to stop all the theorizing and just try to figure out the truth. I realized that in the cases that I won, the reason was not my theory or hypothesis, but the truth.

Many truths have no legal recourse or remedy, even for an injustice. There is also the fear that if we find the truth, it will destroy our case. That's how thinking in terms of evidence and burdens of proof can allow us to avoid the truth if it's not pleasant. Buying into the "I can't know the truth; I just have to make every possible argument to advocate for my client" philosophy may just be a way to avoid confronting the truth.

Uncertainty: The Truth Is Hard to Find

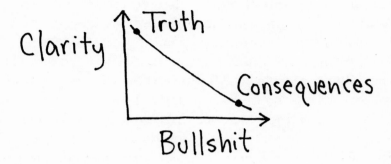

Beyond the natural inclinations that lead lawyers to avoid the truth, there are external factors that get in the way of the truth. While truth is the ultimate goal of cross-examination, absolute scientific truth is not the realm of the lawyer. The lawyer's job is to get as close as possible to the truth, but no one person owns the absolute truth. Especially in cases that go to trial, there is usually a valid disagreement about what happened. Lack of records, photographs, or recordings of what happened creates a void in our ability to know the truth.[4] Into this void clients and witnesses will force a self-serving story or narrative that suits them.

Another obstacle is our society's and juries' acceptance of less than the truth. Princeton philosophy professor Harry G. Frankfurt begins his crudely titled essay "On Bullshit" with the statement, "One of the most salient features of our culture is that there is so much bullshit. Everyone knows this. Each of us contributes

---

[4] In the past thirty years of my career the amount of data available at trials has decreased this void dramatically. E-mails, ubiquitous security cameras, and pervasive data from cell phones, GPS, DNA, and other technologies have greatly increased hard evidence used at trials.

his share."[5] As Frankfurt explains, it is widely accepted in our society for people to speak about things they are not certain of and should not have confidence about. Unfortunately this confidence is persuasive, hiding the absence of facts behind the speaker's statements.

A number of studies have confirmed that juries, especially in complex cases, find expert witnesses persuasive not necessarily on the grounds of their testimony, but on their appearance and speaking skills, including the fluidity and confidence with which they speak.[6] Psychologist Robert Cialdini, in his classic work *Influence: The Psychology of Persuasion,*[7] describes a number of situations where people, even though they rationally understand that what they are doing is based on a falsehood (for example, a weight-loss program that has been scientifically disproven), will nonetheless go ahead when their desire to get what they want is great, or when they are influenced by a persuasive speaker.

So there is a real temptation for the lawyer who does not pursue the truth, but puts forward a case using the tools of persuasion and charisma. The best way to counter those lawyers is to stick with the truth, not try to outcharm and outtrick them. The truth-seeking lawyer has a better chance of winning against the charmer than the theory-based lawyer.

Finally, witnesses exaggerate, evade, misrepresent, falsely claim lack of memory, and otherwise lie all the time, often with the acquiescence, if not the approval,

---

[5] Princeton, NJ: Princeton University Press, 2005, 1.

[6] See, for example, Molly Selvin and Larry Picus, *The Debate over Jury Performance: Observations from a Recent Asbestos Case* (Santa Monica, CA: RAND Corporation, 1987), 27, and Sanja Kutnjak Ivkovic and Valerie P. Hans, "Jurors' Evaluations of Expert Testimony: Judging the Messenger and the Message," *Law and Social Inquiry* 28, no. 2 (Spring 2003).

[7] New York: HarperCollins, 2007.

of lawyers, especially in depositions, where there is no judge to step in and question the testimony. So not only is finding the truth difficult in itself, but it is difficult to overcome active opposition to the truth, which is often allowed or accepted in our legal system.

Famous Truth Finders: Scientist, Detective, Investors, Strategist, and Poet

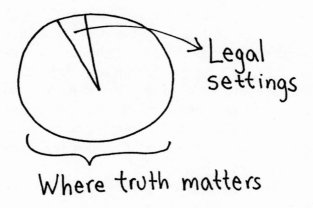

The law itself is not a truth engine. Legal reasoning does not nor is it designed to find truth. So cross-examination exists to fill in what the law is lacking.[8] The kind of thinking that creates good cross-examination is not limited to lawyers, and the best cross-examiners are often thinking outside the legal box. In fact, if you're doing all your thinking in a legal framework, the lawyer with the higher brainpower and clearer logical argument will win. But if you use valid truth-seeking methods from outside the law, you will gain insights and intuition that a person who scored higher than you on the law

---

[8] Systems of law have existed for thousands of years. But as Wigmore suggests in this book's opening epigraph, cross-examination is a more recent invention.

boards might not have. The logic and framework of cross-examination are factual and perceptive, not legal and conceptual. So there is a lot to learn about cross-examination from outside the law.

In my journey to understand the nature of cross-examination, a number of nonlawyers have taught me, through their writings or from reading about them, the thinking methods that are useful in cross-examination. I have chosen these people in particular because I have found myself using their ideas again and again to help me solve a hard trial or cross-examination problem. A full study of their thinking is beyond the scope of this book, but their words describing their thinking have been like signposts to me throughout my career, helping me to see the facts of my cases from a different perspective. Below I present and encourage the reader to learn from a scientist, a detective, two investors, a political and military strategist, and a poet who have much to teach cross-examiners.

The Scientist: Richard Feynman

Richard Feynman (1918–1988) was not only a brilliant physicist and Nobel Prize winner, but also a legendary teacher who could express himself clearly and vividly in his speaking and writing. He proposed several important ideas about critical and scientific thinking that inform this book. The first is to *understand what you know and what you do not*. His statement that the truthful answer to the vast majority of scientific questions is "Nobody knows" is the starting point for me in every case. This statement echoes the Socratic Paradox, "I know one thing: that I know nothing." It means that the only way you can begin to learn the truth is to acknowledge that you are ignorant and then work to find the truth.

The structure of science is similar to that of law in that the scientist starts with a hypothesis (a case theory) suggested by available facts, and then proceeds with an experiment (case investigation), collects data, and presents that data in a peer-reviewed scientific paper (a kind of trial). Scientists, like lawyers, become attached to their hypotheses because they invest a great amount of work and passion in them. The scientific peer-review process—like the adversary system in law—allows other scientists to examine the data and the conclusions drawn from it to subject the work to the best possible critical thinking of the scientific community and to identify flaws like bad data and bad thinking. This is not exactly like a trial but it's a similar process designed to find truth.

Feynman zeroed in on the biggest obstacle for scientists investigating a subject: an unconscious bias that pervades the perception, collection, and selection of data and drawing inferences from it, making scientists lean toward supporting and validating their original hypothesis. The fascinating thing about this bias is that everyone knows about it, yet it persists and again and again taints research results. Similarly, all lawyers would like to believe that they know that the truth is the goal and they believe they base their case on the truth, yet again and again they get blindsided by the truth because they didn't see it.

And so throughout this book we will remind ourselves of this statement that Feynman made in his 1974 commencement address at Caltech: "The first principle is that you must not fool yourself—and you are the easiest person to fool."[9]

The Detective: Sherlock Holmes

Fictional detective Sherlock Holmes, created by Arthur Conan Doyle in the 1880s, is another truth

---

[9] Richard Feynman, *Surely You're Joking, Mr. Feynman! (Adventures of a Curious Character)* (New York: Norton, 1985), 343.

finder whose thinking we want to follow. Holmes is special to me because my father, like Holmes, was also a very good detective. "I'm a cop, not an intellectual like some people around here," he would say, looking in my direction. "I may not be smart, but I have common sense." He was actually very smart and had a great sense of humor. Just as I learned from my dad, cross-examiners can learn more from Sherlock Holmes than from Supreme Court Justice Oliver Wendell Holmes, since cross-examination is a factual art.

Holmes deals in mysteries, crimes, disappearances, and other puzzles that have to be solved. What makes Holmes a master detective and a great literary character, and his stories so interesting, is that he always takes a different view from the obvious surface conclusion. He uses his powerful intellect and deep understanding of human nature to reveal what others cannot see or understand. In every Sherlock Holmes story, what appears at the beginning to be the truth turns out to not be the real truth that he ultimately uncovers. He uses disciplined observation and reasoning to find the real truth while others jump to false conclusions.

Holmes's approach to solving mysteries applies directly to trial work. If your case is going to trial, I guarantee you that hunting for the truth beneath the surface will be fruitful and that the truth you find will not fit your preconceived theory of the case exactly.

Holmes seeks and perceives. He is an acute observer of what is actually in front of his eyes. He uses these accurate perceptions as an inductive thinker. Unlike scientists, he has no hypothesis—in fact he consciously avoids forming a hypothesis in order to keep his perceptions clear.

Holmes also has the skill to separate important details from the irrelevant. Characteristics of important details in his cases are that they connect to a whole, they fit together coherently, and they make sense in the context of his wide body of preexisting general knowledge.

Finally, Holmes never twists the facts to match his conclusion or idea—the most common pitfall of lawyers and the source of many cross-examination failures.

Investors: Warren Buffett and Charlie Munger

In almost no area is finding the truth more important and more rewarding than in investing. And in few areas is it more difficult. The vast majority of individual (as opposed to institutional) investors who engage in securities trading lose money.[10] One reason for this is that people who invest in and trade paper securities have no control over what those stocks do. But emotions (overconfidence, panic, impulsiveness), faulty thinking, and lack of financial education—*all factors within the investor*—compound the lack of control. To see reality in the complex, dynamic financial environment requires highly disciplined thinking. Warren Buffett, one of the wealthiest and most influential people in the world, is an example of a highly successful investor whose success, as he explains in his writings, has come through his contrarian thinking process for seeing things the way others do not.

The psychological and intellectual challenges that investors face have been described by the science of behavioral finance, pioneered by Princeton psychologist Daniel Kahneman.[11] Behavioral finance investigates the pitfalls—such as the tendency to make bad judgments—that otherwise intelligent market actors

---

[10] Brad M. Barber and Terrance Odean, "Trading Is Hazardous to Your Wealth: The Common Stock Investment Performance of Individual Investors," *Journal of Finance* 55, no. 2 (April 2000): 773–806.

[11] See for example Kahneman's *Thinking Fast and Slow* (New York: Farrar, Straus, and Giroux, 2011).

face because of the psychological hard wiring of the brain. Buffett is an example of an investor whose thinking acknowledged and overcame psychological biases even before the science of behavioral finance had fully identified them.

Buffett and his partner Charlie Munger not only think about investing, but think about thinking and how to do it right to get the best results. When they evaluate an investment they attempt to proceed rationally and methodically, relying on hard data. But when they agree that a particular stock or security is a good investment, they distinguish themselves by taking a second step that most investors do not. They examine their methods at every step along the way in order to identify the misjudgments that they *know* they have made. They proceed from the assumption that their emotional desire to make a good investment that will make them money has in fact led them astray in their decision, and they impose a second round of analysis that requires them to identify the thinking errors they have made.

Buffett holds himself to this high standard so that he can see the truth and not delude himself. In a 1999 message to Berkshire Hathaway shareholders, he made an insightful observation about CEOs who cannot see the truth, often because companies are filled with people who tell CEOs what they want to hear: "We will be candid in our reporting to you. . . . We also believe candor benefits us as managers: The CEO who misleads others in public may eventually mislead himself in private."[12]

Buffett also believes that although markets are seduced by short-term emotions, in the end they reflect the truth, and the truth-seer will prevail despite inevi-

---

[12] "Berkshire Hathaway Inc., An Owner's Manual: A Message from Warren E. Buffett, Chairman and CEO," January 1999, http://www.berkshirehathaway.com/owners.html.

table setbacks. In a 1994 letter to his shareholders Buffett quoted economist Benjamin Graham: "In the short-run, the market is a voting machine—reflecting a voter-registration test that requires only money, not intelligence or emotional stability—but in the long-run, the market is a weighing machine."[13] The same is true in legal strategy and cross-examination. Judges and juries may be swayed in the short-term by emotion, charisma, beauty, or prejudice, but in the long run, if you consistently seek the truth, the weight of the truth will make you a winner. Here "weight" means the significance of the truth and connection to other parts of the truth, as well as the influence that weighty facts have on other facts and outcomes.

The Strategist: Themistocles

Themistocles was a Greek general, admiral, and political leader whose grand strategy and uncanny foresight prepared and united the Greek city states (usually at war among themselves) to repel the invasion of the vastly more powerful Persian Empire in the fifth century BCE.

Themistocles is not like the other thinkers above. His thinking is studied far less than that of his compatriot Socrates, whose method is familiar to every lawyer. But I began to look more deeply into his thinking when I read the following quote in the book *The Peloponnesian Wars* by the Athenian general and historian Thucydides:

> Themistocles was a man who showed an unmistakable natural genius; in this respect he was quite exceptional, and beyond all others

---

[13] Letter to the shareholders of Berkshire Hathaway, March 1, 1994, http://www.berkshirehathaway.com/letters/1993.html.

deserves our admiration. Without studying a subject in advance or deliberating over it later, but using simply the intelligence that was his by nature, *he had the power to reach the right conclusion in matters that have to be settled on the spur of the moment and do not admit of long discussions, and in estimating what was likely to happen,* his forecasts of the future were always more reliable than those of others. He could perfectly well explain any subject with which he was familiar, and even outside his own department he was still capable of giving an excellent opinion. *He was particularly remarkable at looking into the future and seeing there the hidden possibilities for good or evil.* To sum him up in a few words, it may be said that through force of genius and rapidity of action *this man was supreme at doing precisely the right thing at precisely the right moment.*[14]

In other words, nobody was better than Themistocles at thinking on his feet in a fast-moving, stressful situation, and yet he thought in terms of long-term strategy. These are the skills that make a great cross-examiner: the ability to quickly size up an unexpected crisis and to see how events will play out in the future; the ability to understand and explain issues both inside and outside one's expertise; the ability to see the good and bad that will come out of any set of facts. Themistocles, better than most people of his time, saw the truth beneath the surface that others could not see, but he knew the truth was hard for people to accept, and that the Athenians and other Greeks would not be

---

[14] Thucydides, *History of the Peloponnesian War*, translated by Rex Warner, rev. ed. (New York: Penguin, 1972), 117; italics added.

inclined to make the hard choices that the truth required. Yet Themistocles was able to lead. How did he do it?

In addition to the qualities that Thucydides described, Themistocles was also a master of deception. He saw the truth and reality, but he never overtly showed his purpose and endgame. Themistocles was one of six generals who fought in the Battle of Marathon in 480 BCE, in which the Athenians threw back a massive Persian invasion. After that victory the Athenians and the other Greeks thought the danger had passed and they went back to their former ways of warring among themselves. But Themistocles saw that an empire with the size, resources, and power of the Persians would not accept a loss and would invade again. He did not let the emotion of a great victory blind his perception of the truth. Thinking in this way, seeing the big picture long term, allowed him to intuitively see how events would probably play out in the future and to know what bets to place on what risks. Thus he persuaded the Athenians to use the profits from public silver mines to build a powerful fleet, the famous "wooden wall" that eventually dealt a final defeat to the next Persian invasion.

As you will see in the coming chapters, this kind of holistic, perceptive, strategic thinking can provide the basis for the quick intuitive questions that are hallmarks of the best cross-examination.

The Poet: Emily Dickinson

Emily Dickinson (1830–1886) is one of America's best-loved poets. Her poetry reflects a rich interior life that grew out of a series of losses of friends and family members who died in the era before modern medicine. These losses, along with her decades of caring for her ill mother, gradually drew her into almost total isolation in the family home in Amherst, Massachusetts, where her main contact with the outside world was through prolific letter writing. She wrote close to 1800 poems but only a few were published during her lifetime.

Dickinson was an outside-the-box poet, so much so that early critics rejected her work for her failure to follow standard conventions of rhyme, meter, capitalization, and punctuation and her use of idiosyncratic words and images. Her earliest published poems were heavily edited to bring them in line with critics' expectations, but by the 1920s her work became viewed as innovative and modern and her popularity grew to almost cult-like proportions. Today she is revered alongside Walt Whitman and Robert Frost.

Most people have read at least some of Dickinson's poems, since they are widely taught in schools. Why should lawyers read her poetry? Because she is a master of expressing the truth with power and brevity in vivid, compact language. Her poetry distills large ideas about life, death, and human nature to their simplest form, using simple, lucid words that surprise and delight. The poems tend to be quite short and often they dispense with titles. Dickinson often dwelt on morbid topics like illness and death, as in one of her most famous untitled poems, which begins:

Because I could not stop for Death —
He kindly stopped for me —
The Carriage held but just Ourselves —
And Immortality.

While scholars have written volumes on the psychological meaning of Dickinson's poems, many can be read as simple and sometimes humorous or ironic reports written in this same brief, direct style, as in the opening lines of "A Bird Came Down the Walk":

A Bird, came down the Walk —
He did not know I saw —
He bit an Angle Worm in halves
And ate the fellow, raw

Emily Dickinson's genius lies in her ability to get at larger truths of life and human emotion in language that can often be understood by school children. She comes at these deep understandings with indirection, stealth, and wit — all elements of great cross-examination that we will discuss. Moreover, her words are memorable, just as you want your words in the courtroom to be memorable. We are drawn to and remember her words, "Because I could not stop for Death, he kindly stopped for me," because they are beautifully and lyrically expressed, they are eminently simple, and they tell a great truth about life and death that grips us instantly, a reminder of our own mortality. All of this is conveyed in just twelve short words!

If you could cross-examine with Dickinson's language and her ability to find and express the truth with power and brevity, you would win more cases, because the judge and jury would be led directly and easily to the central truth that you want them to see. Dickinson's poetry embodies many of the ideas and themes that this book observes are hallmarks of truth finding and truth telling and thus of masterful cross-examination. A master cross-examiner tells a complex story simply and memorably, just as Dickinson does.

If you haven't read any of Dickinson's poems since grade school, I recommend that you return to them now for both the pleasure of reading them and to note her skill for uncovering the truth, her language, and her strategic approach to her subjects.

Principles for Using Truth in Cross-Examination

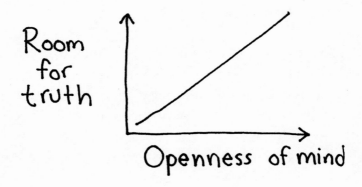

Room for truth

Openness of mind

I hope I have convinced you that finding and revealing the truth is the best approach to cross-examination. I believe that at the center of every case there is a truth. It is the center of gravity, the quiet eye of the hurricane. It is the place where the best cross-examinations come from, and from that, the best trial strategy, tactics, and conduct. But how do you find and reveal the truth in practice? I suggest that you start with the following principles:

1. *When you get a new case, look for the truth at its center.* Base your case on the truth, rather than a theory that helps you win.

2. *Identify how your client is biased, short sighted, exaggerating, or misleading you* and follow those clues to figure out the truth.

3. *Accept that the truth is always uncertain, hidden, and unclear, but always try to get closer to it.* Understand that the "whole truth" is unknowable for most practical purposes. The most plausible truth will work.

4. *Remember that the truth is unstable.* Very often what you thought were facts will change. Not only facts themselves but context, perspective, and emotion can change the truth from what was thought to be certain before.

5. *Recognize that the legal adversarial system is a flawed way to find the truth.* It requires a lawyer to make a winning case based on incomplete information, and inclines the lawyer to truth blindness and thinking errors. Generally, the truth is outside the box of legal thinking.

6. *Assume that the truth is not the narrative that you originally devise.* Assume that your case theory misses the truth in some way. In hard cases, the truth will be off center from the case theories of both sides. You will be a better cross-examiner if you seek to understand and occupy the high ground of the truth before your adversary. This often happens during trial and not before.

7. *Cross-examine only on what you know to be true or what you know to be false.* Only fight the battles you can win and focus on what is most important.

CHAPTER SUMMARY

Main Takeaway

Seeing the big truth, the whole truth in a case is difficult and cloudy. But there are smaller truths that you can know, and the best cross-examinations build from these.

Earthquake Points

When I prepare to cross-examine, I always create several "earthquake points." If there were an earthquake during my questioning, what one question would I ask before I ran out of the courthouse? At the end of each chapter I will give you some points you can turn to if there is an earthquake and you can't read the whole chapter.

- Cross-examination is asking questions that reveal the truth.

- Finding the truth is a process of gathering facts and evidence, drawing inferences from them, and assembling them into a narrative story of your case.

- The truth is the best case and cross-examination strategy because it will help you succeed in more cases.

- Truth is not absolute; it is uncertain.

- The lawyer who seeks the truth and bases case strategy on it has the advantage. Look for the truth before formulating arguments about your case.

- Deception and falsehood are attractive when they seem to bolster your case. Don't be trapped by them. Examine the evidence critically and skeptically. Recognize your inherent bias and thinking flaws.

- To get to the truth you need to see your whole case, the big picture. Then each of your small decisions can be framed in relation to the whole case.

CHAPTER 2

ALL THINGS ARE MADE OF ATOMS

Facts as the Basic Building Blocks of Cross-Examination

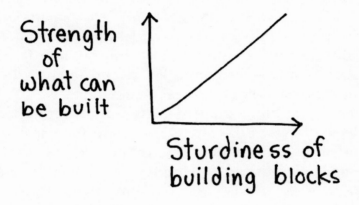

If, in some cataclysm, all of scientific knowledge were to be destroyed, and only one sentence passed on to the next generations of creatures, what statement would contain the most information in the fewest words? I believe it is the *atomic hypothesis* (or the atomic fact, or whatever you wish to call it) that *all things are made of atoms—little particles that move around in perpetual motion, attracting each other when they are a little distance apart or repelling upon being squeezed into one another.* In that one sentence, you will see, there is an enormous amount of information about the world, if just a little imagination and thinking were applied.

—Richard Feynman, *Lectures on Physics*

Richard Feynman's question, "What statement would contain the most information in the fewest words?" is a trial lawyer's question. Lawyers build on primary or basic elements of truth just as scientists build an entire body of scientific knowledge by making inferences from a solitary atom. Cross-examination, like experimental science, is a rational art that tries to find the truth by pulling out information from its most fundamental elements. For scientists, the primary element is the atom; for lawyers, it's the fact.

Facts are the primary material and foundation of all legal things. Like atoms, facts are the most basic elements of information that cannot be cut, sanded, stripped, or reduced to simpler parts. Just as everything in the world is made of atoms, every legal case, every human event, or set of actions that created a legal dispute is made of facts. To master cross-examination is to master the art of facts. The master cross-examiner begins each case by searching for basic facts, and develops each case by continuing that search. Masters of cross-examination are masters of facts.

A number of writers have stated rules and principles of cross-examination, but to be a great cross-examiner, you must go beyond rules and prescribed approaches and seek the truth that lies in the facts underlying every legal conflict. These simple and most basic facts are the atoms from which cases are made.

To illustrate these points, let's look at a fictional police report recording an eyewitness account of two defendants leaving the scene of a shooting and robbery at a convenience store.

> Mr. Crane, 40 years old, lives across the street from the robbed premises. Was in his front room, heard a screech, and through his window observed two young men getting in a green convertible and driving west on Jefferson St. Mr. Crane observed the perpetrators from a distance of 75 feet. Positively identified both perpetrators.

In the above example the police report is filled with what appear to be facts. The witness is a man. He is forty years old. He lives across the street from the convenience store that was robbed. He was in his home at the time. He saw two young men leaving the premises and saw them drive away in a green convertible. However, these facts have not been *atomized*. An atomized fact has been reduced to its most fundamental parts that provide data to the inductive thinker, like the detective who searches out the meaningful fact that will lead to more knowledge about the case and eventually the truth of what occurred.

This simple case presents an opportunity to compare two different styles of thinking and problem solving: deductive and inductive. Detectives seek the truth inductively, which means that they first locate the facts and then figure out the truth from the facts. The best detectives are willing to spend large amounts of time and effort to find just one simple fact. Like a bloodhound, they will fixate on a single but important fact and are willing to follow alleyways to every door and haystack until they find the one fact they're looking for.

Lawyers, however, are trained to be deductive thinkers: they begin with concepts, theories, or hypotheses and then try to verify these abstract theories with facts. They begin with the law and apply the facts to the law. Lawyers love concepts, abstraction, and arguments. They spend three years in law school studying documents that have preselected facts to support arguments. Few lawyers get an education in finding or learning facts, or in distinguishing true facts from their many alternatives. In law school, the best students are selected for law review. No law school has "fact review." Consequently, lawyers wrongly pursue theories rather than facts. They have it backwards—facts lead to the truth. In their enthusiasm for argument and for putting forth their side of the case, lawyers sometimes ignore or undervalue a fact that just doesn't quite fit their concept of the case. However, the fact that the detective is willing to sweat for and that the arguing lawyer is willing to ignore is an indisputable and key element of the case.

But there is also uncertainty. Is the witness to the fleeing suspects mistaken? Is his mind fooling him into believing he remembers what he does not? Has his mind reconstructed or completed things he did not actually see, perhaps influenced by the type of questions the police asked? What is the probability that he really saw what the report concludes he saw?

If you're an inductive thinker, you may conclude, based on the facts in the police report alone, that this witness is useless. Or you may decide the exact opposite, depending on whether you represent the prosecution or the defense. The point is, you have not yet atomized these facts and discovered the truth embedded in the deeper facts that have not yet been uncovered. You are drawing conclusions and potentially losing the case. The more time and intellectual effort you spend trying to find the fundamental facts of your case, the deeper your understanding of the case will be, and the more powerful your cross-examination questions will be. Any lawyer can make the facts conform to a particular concept of the case, but masterful lawyers modify their concept of the case to conform to the facts.

What Are Facts, Anyway?

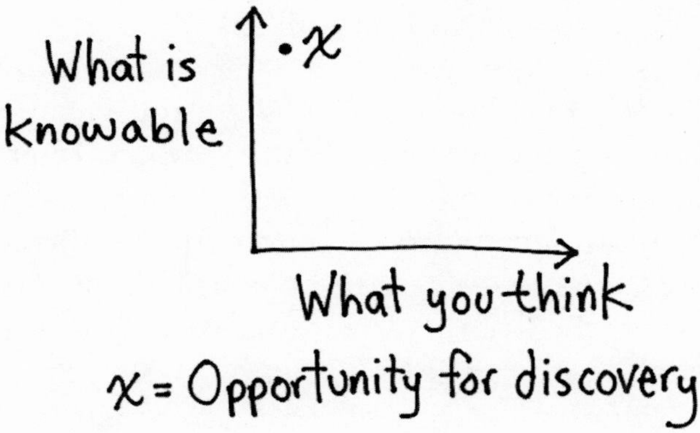

What is knowable $\uparrow$ • x

What you think →

x = Opportunity for discovery

A fact is a simple, concrete, undisputed statement of what happened or did not happen. A fact is a statement that can be proven true or false. After that, there is disagreement. The Oxford Dictionary defines a fact as "a thing that is indisputably the case." Your problem is trying to figure out and state something in a way that cannot reasonably be disputed. That's good as far as it goes, but you can be sure that opponents in a legal case are going to disagree on what the facts are. Francis Bacon defined facts as those things that can be objectively proven. Trial lawyers should only consider facts that fit Bacon's or the dictionary definition. They are simple descriptions of objects, persons, relationships, and so on. A fact is not reality itself, but a short statement that tries its best to describe reality.

33

Facts are not opinions, exaggerations, statements that appear to be facts but have in them embedded opinions or conclusions, spin, or anything else that can reasonably be disputed by your adversary. Sometimes there is more than one version of the simple, concrete statements of what happened or did not happen; such varying statements are "disputed facts." The starting point of all cross-examination is to focus on the simplest, most provable, undisputed facts. If a fact is not in dispute, a good cross-examiner will ask about it and firmly establish it. The light was red? There is no doubt about that? The light was not green? The light was definitely not yellow? We have established a simple, concrete fact that the light was red.

I call another category of statements nonfacts. These are abstractions like descriptive characteristics that we believe are facts. Characterizations are opinions embedded in such words as "big," "fast," "good," or "bad." A cross-examiner must be able to distinguish facts from nonfacts.

So we begin to gather facts about our witness, Mr. Crane. We know he does in fact live across the street from the place that was robbed. His house in fact has a window that faces the convenience store, which is in fact roughly a distance of seventy-five feet from the front of Mr. Crane's house. All of these are facts. But who he saw, what he saw, and whether two youths were fleeing are not facts. Not yet, anyway. Nonfacts are important in cross-examination. In any contest, such as a trial, political campaign, or business negotiation, people will try to put up nonfacts as facts. You yourself will do it without realizing it.

A good cross-examiner delights in facts, is cautious about nonfacts, and avoids inferences and conclusions altogether. Inferences that are drawn from facts are also nonfacts, unless the inference is indisputable—which it rarely is—or unless the witness agrees to the inference. Conclusive statements—broad arguments from both facts and inferences—are also nonfacts as they are even more abstract than inferences. Based on what we know about Mr. Crane from the police report and the new facts we've uncovered, the master cross-examiner—an inductive and atomizing lawyer—cannot yet conclude whether Mr. Crane saw anything relevant to the crime and would be foolish to infer or conclude anything at this point. The master cross-examiner has not yet seen all of the facts.

Seeing the Truth with the Right Brain

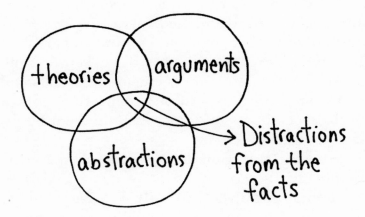

The ability to see facts clearly and objectively is an enormous advantage in cross-examination. The lawyer who can see the simple facts of the case will have the advantage over the vast majority of lawyers, who approach cases by looking for any scrap of information—fact or not—that supports their preconceived conclusions about the case. But like the atoms described by Feynman, the facts of a legal case are in constant motion, changing and recombining with new information and different understandings of their context and characterizations by different parties. It is a constant job to see the facts. You cannot simply find them and expect that they will be there for you unchanged at trial.

Everyone thinks they know what facts are, but when you hear lawyers asking questions or making arguments in court, what they call facts are often opinions, characterizations, theories, concepts, or abstractions. Many lawyers call arguments facts. But a master cross-examiner can *see* facts and articulate them clearly without any embellishment. The abstract-thinking mind of a lawyer advocating a case creates models of facts from ideas rather than observing facts in the real world and recording them truthfully. This fallacy is called the "Bed of Procrustes," after a mythical giant who captured his victims and tied them to a bed. If they couldn't fit in the bed, he would pound and crush their limbs with a hammer until they did. The great pitfall of lawyers is to think that conclusions are facts and to crush the facts until they fit into their arguments. Perceive the facts; don't infer or conclude them by using logic or argument.

The book *Drawing on the Right Side of the Brain*[1] by Betty Edwards describes the tendency of the left brain to conceptualize rather than truly see. The book gives an example of the left brain actually interfering with people seeing what is right in front of them, their own hand. When untrained people are told to draw their own hand, they don't draw what they see, but instead draw an abstract idea of a hand. According to Dr. Edwards, this is because they draw using their left brain, rather than their right brain.[2]

---

[1] New York: Tarcher/Penguin, 2012.

Lawyers are left brained. The left brain, the brain you spend three years in law school training, is uncomfortable looking at the real world, because the left brain delights in models, abstractions, and theories—the stuff of legal briefs. Thus the left brain wants you to draw your hand like a plastic surgical glove that has been used as a balloon with none of the defining features of a real hand. The abstract idea of a hand isn't real and doesn't look like any real hand. If you build your case using abstract words and ideas, and if you cross-examine using abstractions, your case will be no more real a picture of the facts to the jury than a distorted, flat drawing of an idea of a hand.

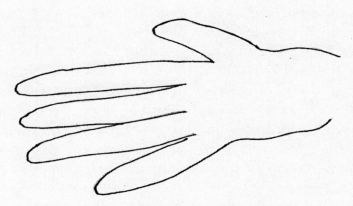

My left-brain abstract drawing of a hand.

---

[2] Recent scientific studies cast doubt on whether these modes of thinking are actually located in the physical left or right hemisphere. See for example Tania Lambrozo, "The Truth about the Left Brain/Right Brain Relationship," National Public Radio, December 2, 2013, http://www.npr.org/sections/13.7/2013/12/02/248089436/the-truth-about-the-left-brain-right-brain-relationship. But the metaphor of left brain/right brain differences is embedded in our way of talking about thinking styles, so I am using it here to distinguish perceptual thinking (right brain) from conceptual thinking (left brain).

If you want to be a master cross-examiner, you have to cast away the logic, abstraction, and theory that you were taught in left-brain law school and enter the world of clear, factual, right-brain observation. Cross-examination is not taught very much in law school because it is not compatible with conventional legal thinking. When you were taught to "think like a lawyer," you were not taught to carefully observe facts. Instead, you were taught to choose facts that fit the argument you're promoting and to minimize or ignore facts that don't serve that argument.

But when you simply observe facts, without trying to make them fit into what you assume or want to argue, and without judging them according to how well they serve your preconceived assumptions, you have taken the first step on the path to mastery as a cross-examiner. When you learn to shut down your left brain, your arguing brain, and see what your hand really looks like and draw it from your actual observations without interference from abstraction, you can draw a hand that looks human, real, believable: the actual lines, edges, contours, and spaces that make up the image of the hand with no abstract conceptions distorting the image. Master cross-examiners think perceptively, not conceptually.

This act of fact *seeking* and fact *seeing* is the kind of inductive reasoning identified by the great lawyer Francis Bacon, known as empiricism. Bacon's approach was to find and identify facts and to measure them objectively. Only once you have established the data do you attempt to infer the meaning or significance of the facts. Not surprisingly, this thinking is the basis for the scientific method and is the best starting point for cross-examinations.

If you have practiced this kind of thinking—looking for and perceiving facts clearly and without bias—

My more realistic right-brain drawing of a hand.

it will carry through when you must stand and confront a witness in cross-examination. You will have the edge because you will see the facts truly and ask questions from the strength of the facts. Your worldview will be factual and real. Your questioning will come out of this mind-set, and your questions will be more real and factual.

Returning to my initial analogy about facts and atoms, keep in mind that, like atoms, not all facts are visible to the naked eye. Scientists must use effort and scientific analysis to get at the atomic structure of the material world. The same is true for the facts of your case. But once you have successfully atomized your case, you will have important advantages over an adversary who has not used this approach.

First, you will understand what is real and what is not, what can be attacked and disputed and what cannot. Second, you will command the basic facts outside a model, argument, or story. You will have examined the simple and most basic underlying facts without being committed to a theory, argument, defense, or claim. This gives you the flexibility of understanding and perception that you will need to be a master cross-examiner. It gives you a chance to see the truth—which is not always the conclusion that you wanted to see. By not being rigidly bound to how you can use each of the facts, you can put them together to make or not make inferences. Further, you will know when the witness is committing violations of rationality by claiming that an opinion, argument, or assumption is a fact when it is not.

Just as important, you will be able to recognize when things you thought were facts turn out not to be. As Greek philosopher Heraclitus said, "Into the same river you could not step twice, for other waters are flowing." As in science, your search for facts is never ending and constantly revised by new information and new context. Witnesses can change their testimony. Other witnesses that you have not talked to could credibly contradict your witness. Anomalous or eccentric facts could be put into context or explained, and what seemed important becomes irrelevant or vice versa. Like atoms, the facts are always in motion, always in play. That is why time and effort spent in the early parts of the case trying to break things down to their most fundamental elements and figure out what is real will pay dividends later.

Simple Words

In objective-based fields of study like science or finance, facts are stated as numbers, but for the trial of

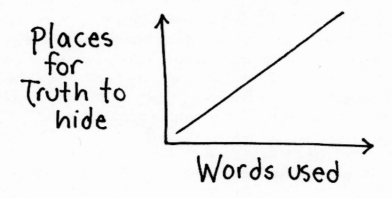

a case and for cross-examination we must state facts in words, which almost always carry subjective weight. In cross-examination, the lawyer uses words to make questions about facts. Each of these elements—words, questions, and facts—must be distilled to their most precise meaning, and when you are cross-examining a witness you must employ the most straightforward and simplest words that closely reflect the indisputability of the facts without intermediation of concept, argument, or opinion. It is a constant effort to distill facts into their simplest statements. Like entropy, there is constant erosion of precision and clarity with more words, especially words that are more conceptual and less concrete. There is constant slippage that distorts simple facts as they are put together or told in a narrative.

These simple and precise words that are the bricks and mortar of your questions are found in the physical world, where the real events underlying a case happened. The best cross-examination words are short, concrete, and vivid. These words percolate up from the groundwork you have done in your investigation. Like a writer, a master cross-examiner finds the unique words that communicate the essence of the case.

These words are the precise words (as opposed to jargon) used by the people involved in the events of the case. When you interview your client and witnesses, listen closely to their language. Take down their very words. Do not let your thinking get between the facts you learn and the questions you make. For example, read the following questioning of Mr. Crane:

Q: Mr. Crane, why don't you tell us what happened.

A: I was watching Jerry Springer when I heard a screech.

Q: You saw the guys come out of the convenience store?

A: Yes.

Q: Where were you when you saw them?

A: I was standing in my front room looking out the window.

Q: You were close enough to get a good look?

A: Sure was.

Mr. Crane's words are the raw material of cross-examination. His precise words from the police report and his statement—"screech," "green convertible," "front room," and "window"—will become some of the facts in your case. But there are also nonfacts: "good look" and "saw the guys" not only are conclusions but may be influenced by suggestive police questions. All of these facts, like atoms and matter, are building the real world of your case.

Facts Make Stories

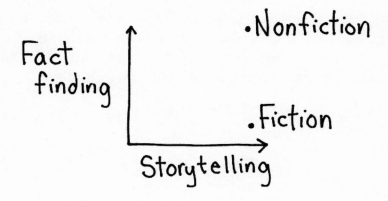

Lawyers call the story of their case the "theory of the case," but I don't like that phrase because it isn't concrete enough. A case should be a vivid, tactile story that a jury can see, hear, touch, smell, and experience. Never say to a jury, "This is my theory of the case." I have heard lawyers use these words many times. Lawyers make the common mistake of creating a theory because they think a legal conclusion will win the case. Facts must create the case, not logic or concepts. Disasters happen when you construct the theory first and then go off in search of facts. Don't adopt the theory; let the theory come to you inductively from the facts that you have learned from your investigation. The facts will tell you the truth and, when you truly see them, the facts will suggest the inferences and explanations that make the best presentation of your case. It is a *bad* theory that contradicts a significant fact. *Cross-examination is important because it is a process of facts defeating theory.* Somebody's theory of the case is going to topple when struck by the facts of a good cross-examination. A story built on facts can better withstand an assault.

Let's return to our convenience store robbery and shooting. Based on the police report alone, we could theorize that Mr. Crane is an identifying eyewitness to the crime. But the cross-examiner's atomized list of facts may tell a different story. When we take apart the police report and interview and reduce them to their basic elements, we get a list something like this:

> convenience store
>
> youths
>
> green
>
> convertible
>
> leaving
>
> fast
>
> street
>
> distance
>
> lawn
>
> porch
>
> fence
>
> porch furniture
>
> window
>
> open, closed?
>
> screen
>
> inside furniture
>
> couch
>
> television

When you go over these bits of information, something magical happens. Arguments, inferences, and ideas begin to bubble up from the simple facts that lie on the floor before you like Lego blocks. Listing the elemental facts highlights the nonfacts and helps you notice and define them. The facts and nonfacts contrast against one another.

Looking at both the police narrative and the interview, the most pertinent nonfacts for our example are:

"observed" (2 times)

"identified"

"saw"

"fleeing"

"good look"

The good cross-examiner perceives what are facts and where facts may be missing. He (in this case the lawyer is a man) goes to the scene and slowly, with his camera in hand, walks around every part of it. He consciously tries to perceive every detail, every atom. He goes to the convenience store, inspects the parking area and the street to see if there are tire marks, goes across the street to Mr. Crane's house, crosses Mr. Crane's front lawn, and goes up the steps to Mr. Crane's front porch, all the while taking pictures of everything, and then goes right up to the window from which Mr. Crane "saw," "observed," and "got a good look" at the youths. Then, having found or observed the simple facts, and discarding those facts that were not absolutely essential, the lawyer at trial conducts the following cross-examination:

Q: Hey, Mr. Crane, what are these pictures of?

A: My house and stuff.

Q: Your house and stuff. And what is this brown stuff on the windows?

A: Dirt.

Q: Dirt? What is this rusty, dusty, dirty-looking thing over your window?

A: It's a screen.

Q: A screen? It's a screen. And what are these big things right in the middle of your view, from the middle of your window to the Sack O' Suds? What do we call these big things?

A: Trees?

Q: Trees, that's right. Don't be afraid. Just shout 'em right out when you know 'em. Now, what are these thousands of little things that are on trees?

A: Leaves?

Q: And these bushy things between the trees?

A: Bushes?

Q: Bushes, right. So, Mr. Crane, you could positively identify the defendants for a moment of two seconds looking through this dirty window, this crud-covered screen, these trees with all these leaves on them, and I don't know how many bushes.

A: Looks like five.

Q: Ah ah, don't forget this one and this one.

A: Seven bushes.

Q: So, what do you think? Do you think it's possible you just saw two guys in a green convertible, and not necessarily these two particular guys?

A: I suppose.

Gambini: I'm finished with this guy.[3]

You may recognize this cross-examination from the movie *My Cousin Vinny*, which is one of the most accurate film depictions of courtroom techniques, especially the questioning of witnesses.[4] If you listen to the answers to attorney Vinny Gambini's questions, you see the atoms, the simple hard facts expressed clearly in concrete words, that Vinny uses to push away and contradict the nonfacts in the police report and interview:

"my house and stuff"

"dirt"

"it's a screen"

"trees"

"leaves"

"bushes"

"looks like five"

"seven bushes"

---

[3] Assistant Dean Andrew Rossner of Rutgers Law School uses this example in his lectures on cross-examination.

[4] Another example is the scene where Vinny's girlfriend, played by Marisa Tomei, testifies as an expert witness in auto mechanics. This scene shows flawless technique in both stating the legal qualifications for an expert witness and in the expert testimony itself.

Vinny designed each question (except the final one, which was risky, but an acceptable risk) to allow only one short, simple answer. As an aside, the questions do not sound like traditional leading questions that cross-examination teachers tell us to use, which state a fact and ask for agreement or not. Vinny uses the pictures to control the witness and ask the (slightly sarcastic) questions without sounding like a lawyer.

Should a criminal defense lawyer pursue the truth on cross-examination? There is an argument, even endorsed by some courts, that criminal defense lawyers need not adhere to the truth in their questioning on cross-examination. But I believe that the truth is the strongest strategy in any situation where the truth is knowable. The above cross-examination adheres strictly to the facts and the truth and is highly effective. I find that lawyers want to stray from the truth because it's easier to make an argument without digging for the truth. But the scene from *My Cousin Vinny* is an excellent example of finding the truth and using the atoms of the truth to raise a reasonable doubt in a criminal case.

None of these questions would have come to mind (or have been brought to the attention of the jury) had the facts in the police report not been atomized. We now have a very different picture of the events — a more real, although less certain picture. This is because we uncovered and saw the simplest and most irreducible facts in the case, saw each fact clearly, without preconception, and articulated the facts in clear, precise words.

Only after digging deeply and perceiving the most basic facts did we begin to look for what the facts signified. The story that then told itself was more real and more true.

How does this process of breaking the case into its smallest parts promote excellent cross-examination? It encodes in your mind simple, real, discrete facts. The time that you spend in quiet, clarifying and settling the facts and breaking them into atoms, will put the facts in your memory in the same form that you will use at trial and in cross-examination. You will also have found and separated out nonfacts, so that you will avoid them yourself, but will recognize and respond correctly to them when the witness answers with a nonfact. You will be able to choose to cross-examine where you know there are facts, and avoid areas where there are no facts or insufficient facts. Your mind can, in the stressful and quickly changing contest that is cross-examination, instantly make these atoms into short, simple, power-ful, vivid questions that make great cross-examination.

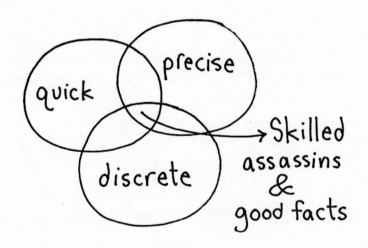

CHAPTER SUMMARY

Main Takeaway

Cross-examination is an art of facts. Facts, not theories, win cases, and your indisputable facts can defeat your adversary's case built on theory. To master cross-examination is to master the art of facts.

Earthquake Points

- Facts are the most basic elements—the atoms—of a case.

- A fact is a statement that can be proven to be true objectively.

- Theories, abstractions, characterizations, inferences, and conclusions are nonfacts unless they can be proven.

- Facts lead to the truth, so pursue facts rather than your theory of the case. Modify your concept of the case to conform to the facts.

- To discover the truth hidden in facts, you must "atomize" them by reducing them to their most fundamental parts.

- Begin your cross-examination by establishing the undisputed, most provable facts.

- Seek and see the facts; don't infer or conclude them by using logic or argument.

- The facts of a case are always in motion as

the case evolves. Knowing the facts of your case will allow you to use them flexibly as the case changes.

- In cross-examining a witness use the most straightforward and simplest words—short, concrete, and vivid—to get to the indisputable facts, without argument or opinion.

- Word each question to allow only one short answer.

CHAPTER 3

BIG FACTS WIN CASES

Disasters averted

Attention paid to facts of the matter

FROM THE MANY CASES I HAVE TRIED, I have learned that the judge or jury most often base their decision on the main facts of the case, the ones I knew about on the first day I took the case. Even in massive, complex cases, it is often the large, simple, and indisputable Big Facts that determine the outcome of the case, despite the existence of millions of documents and hundreds of witnesses. I have sometimes, through blindness or stubbornness, refused to accept this. After having been whacked in the head with this phenomenon dozens of times, I reached a fundamental truth I call *Karam's Maxim*: Big Facts Win Cases.

On January 8, 1986, the space shuttle Challenger disintegrated moments after takeoff, tragically killing all seven crew members on board. In the aftermath of the disaster, NASA had to not only explain what went wrong and why, but justify the need for an on-

53

going space program. It was a public relations nightmare. In response to NASA's predicament, physicist Richard Feynman observed, "For a successful technology, reality must take precedence over public relations, for nature cannot be fooled."[1] Feynman's insight that facts determine outcome underscores my point that Big Facts are the reality of the case whether in nature or in the courtroom. Avoidance of the Big Facts—an unwillingness to face up to them—amounts to a failure of critical thinking. Any story based on an unwillingness to accept Big Facts is a failed story. I know this. Yet I confess that when a Big Fact has been against me, I have sometimes spent a tremendous amount of time, effort, and brainpower—all limited resources—trying to deny it, explain it away, or rationalize it. Accepting Big Facts is a struggle in every case.

In your search for Big Facts, you must be aware of the danger of blindly accepting your client's version of the facts or assessment of what facts are important. Some lawyers advise that you interview your client and then craft a theory that allows the facts your client has provided you to satisfy the legal requirements of a claim or defense. I strongly disagree with this method. Often the client's theory is not the right theory because clients invariably leave out important facts that are negative or that put them in a bad light. You must independently investigate the facts and let the facts tell you the story.

When confronted with a new case, your first task is to identify the Big Facts. This requires critical thinking, a form of analysis that challenges, questions, and evaluates all of the information you receive. Through this process, the Big Facts inevitably emerge and become

---

[1] Richard P. Feynman, "Personal Observations on the Reliability of the Shuttle," in *What Do You Care What Other People Think? Further Adventures of a Curious Character.* New York: W.W. Norton, 1988.

the foundation of your case or story that will serve you throughout your case, from your pleadings to your summation. A story that correctly and truthfully sets out the Big Facts without argument or conclusion will earn you the judge's respect and will be a headache to your adversary. And with the Big Facts to guide you, your cross-examination is clearer and easier. This is because sticking to the Big Facts is a core practice of the principle of *simplicity*. Simplicity is of paramount importance in complex cases. It gives you the high ground and advantage, because you can quickly get to the point that the judge and jury want. These points lie close to the Big Facts and flow from them.

What Are Big Facts?

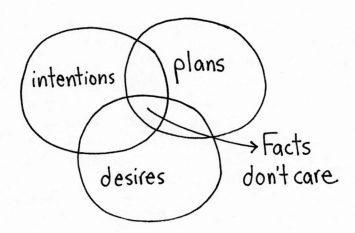

Big Facts are anchored in the physical world. In criminal cases, guns, clothing, blood, fingerprints, and photographs form the material basis for Big Facts. Counterintuitively, Big Facts may not be immediately obvious. Sometimes the Big Facts are physically small, for example a letter or a signature that doesn't look right. A scuff on a shoe. A shadow in a photograph. In civil cases, the physical evidence is contracts, bills of receipt, X-rays, meeting minutes, bank statements. If money is involved, and it usually is, who got the money is a Big Fact. Lawyers since the time of Cicero and probably before have asked, "Cui Bono?" or "Who benefited?" This is the same sentiment expressed by Deep Throat, the confidential source during the Watergate scandal, when he said, "Follow the money."

Many facts may seem neutral, but if you can connect neutral facts you may find that they form or at least lead to a Big Fact, or just as important, undermine what your adversary puts up as a Big Fact. The best trial lawyers are open to unexpected and unforeseen facts that the opponent has not contested or may not be aware of, and use these to support or undermine Big Facts in the case.

Let's return to our stalwart witness to a robbery and murder, Mr. Crane. The prosecution has a number of seemingly favorable facts from Mr. Crane's testimony that support his theory. Mr. Crane was looking out his front window shortly after the crime; he saw two young men leave the convenience store and drive quickly away in a green convertible. The prosecution claimed to have a Big Fact—an eyewitness identification. But the defense attorney uncovered other facts, unexpected and small details, that the prosecutor could not dispute: dirt and a cruddy screen on the window; seven bushes in front of the window. These facts allowed the defense to generate a case story that showed that Mr. Crane had an obstructed view and could not clearly see the faces of the young men as they drove away. What the prosecutor believed to be a Big Fact was not, because important small facts convincingly undermined what appeared to be a Big Fact. As we discussed earlier, the truth is hard to find but Big Facts are always in the neighborhood of the truth.

How to Recognize Big Facts

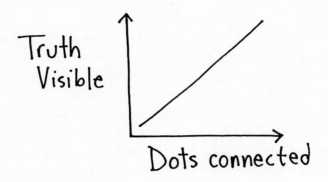

Like most lawyers who are analytical by nature and often driven competitively to run down every last detail in a case, I sometimes lose sight of the power of Big Facts. I agonize over details and search for every possible relevant fact that supports my case. And though the process of *seeking* and *seeing* the facts of the case story is important, as previously discussed, every lawyer knows that some facts are more important than others. The measure of whether a fact is important, or Big, is the number of strong inferences that flow from the proof of that fact. If a certain fact is true, a number of others must follow or else defy common sense and credibility. If every fact in your case is an atom, then Big Facts are like the organic atoms of carbon, hydrogen, and oxygen. They draw the highest number of other atoms to themselves and generate the most numerous and powerful molecular compounds. Big Facts compel the truth of a large number of details and lesser facts.

Like time and brainpower, cross-examination is a limited resource. Your cross-examination should stay close to the Big Facts. The only lesser facts you should be concerned about are those that support the truth of Big Facts or that derive their truth from Big Facts. Big Facts are central to the case; they are indisputable and generate all other small facts and inferences relevant to the case.

Take the case of a housing developer who sued his contractor for breach of contract, in particular, breach of a condition that required that the property be "habitable," a term that neither party adequately defined. After the tenants moved in, all kinds of problems arose: toilets weren't fastened to the floor; air conditioning systems were too weak for the space; windows were stuck; lights flickered; mold appeared; and consequently leases were terminated. The contractor stuck to his Big Fact: everything was built to code and he had the permits and approvals to prove it. The builder had his Big Fact too: he couldn't get anyone to live in his building. He had other facts as well, smaller ones that orbited around the Big Fact: people won't live in a building that doesn't have a working toilet, that's too hot, that smells. From that, the fact finder was able to infer that the building

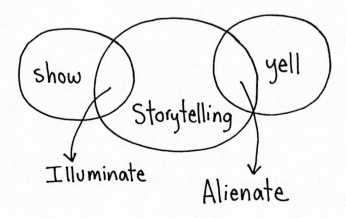

was not habitable, a material breach of the contract. An unspoken truth is that building inspectors often look the other way on code violations when it suits them, and pass buildings they shouldn't pass.

The Path of Least Resistance

The facts you uncover create the story of your case. These are the facts that are the basis of your cross-examination questions and that you will bring together in your summation as your complete case story. If throughout this process you focus on the Big Facts, your story as well as your cross-examination and summation will be on a path of least resistance that will lead the jury to agree with your conclusion.

You should not cross-examine on disputed facts. Lawyers spend a lot of time fighting about facts. But cross-examining about disputed facts is not the best use of your limited cross-examination time. Jurors, on the other hand, hate to resolve disputed factual issues. They feel like a parent trying to figure out which of their kids started the latest fight. They don't want to be in the middle of a squabble.

If you lose the jurors, you lose your case. Fighting over facts with the opposition is like starting and stopping a good joke to get a small detail right: it inhibits the flow of the narrative and makes it difficult for your audience or jury to understand the inherent power of the case story.

In the case of the builder against his contractor, the builder's attorney avoided a tedious argument about the intended meaning of the word "habitable" as being applicable to either building standards only or, as the builder understood it, the small details of daily living. Instead, the builder's attorney showed the jury the facts:

the slow drain, the unusable kitchen light, the backward switch, the failure of the air conditioning to significantly lower the air temperature after forty minutes. Each accumulated fact built a path to one conclusion: no one could live in the building. Simple and direct, a path of least resistance.

Big Bad Facts

Big Facts often are the very cause of the case: someone was murdered; the company went bankrupt. They come from hard evidence like documents, test results, laws of nature, and so on. These are facts that are hard to dispute, which is not to say that you never should try to do so. Sometimes, disputing an inconvenient or incriminating fact—a Big Bad Fact—is your only chance to help your client. For example, a common defense tactic in criminal trials is to dispute that the police recovered evidence from your client. The defense says, "No, they lied, the evidence was not actually on my client."

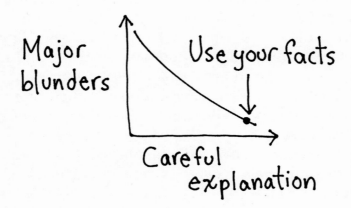

Everything depends on the jury accepting the defense's denial of the police's source of evidence. If the jury rejects the denial, the client goes down. You need to understand that this is a high-risk strategy.

A better strategy is to turn the tide on a Big Fact without frontally disputing it by changing the inferences that a jury draws from the Big Fact. I have defended many criminal cases where logic provided no viable defense and the client refused my advice to plead guilty. I have learned to accept the Big Bad facts and to investigate and offer alternative facts. By doing so, I try to show that the Big Bad Fact is completely consistent with my case story, as when a seemingly damning fact can be characterized as a usual habit, a triviality not even relevant to this case. For example, your client is placed at the scene of the crime. However, you have uncovered the fact that he actually passes by that very spot on his walk home from work every night. You did not change the fact—your client was indeed at the scene of the crime—but you changed the inference that his presence at that place is an indication of his guilt to an inference that he was merely where he always is.

Use Big Facts to Cross-Examine

Big Facts compel more numerous and more powerful inferences than other facts. Inferences come from groups of facts together. You can make up inference bundles as you prepare your case, and then cross-examine to elicit these facts together, leaving off any questions about the inference itself. Unassailable inferences are a matter of probability, but here is where you can use Aristotelian syllogisms—in which a conclusion is inferred from two or more premises—to make tight bricks of hard facts, joined together by the mortar of

61

strong inferences. Most lawyers recognize and understand syllogisms, since they are the essence of the left-brain logical thinking that makes up legal thinking. The classic syllogism is "All men are mortal. Socrates is a man. Therefore Socrates is mortal." Simple, big, unassailable facts. Tight undeniable logic. When the Big Facts are on your side, the need for intuitive and tactical thinking recedes. You have strength on your side, so there is no need for deception, for flanking movements. You use simple facts and logic to engage in a direct assault.

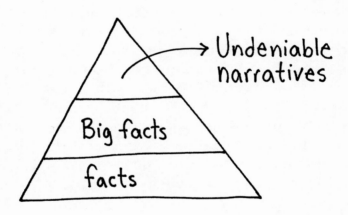

A tactic of cross-examination is to ask a witness to make an inference that the witness cannot credibly deny, such as the builder's attorney asking the contractor whether he would live in a house without functioning toilets. The risk in this tactic is that the witness might respond with a reasonable inference, bad for your case, that you have not thought of. So make sure there are no other credible inferences. What can the contractor possibly answer to that question that will help him? The witness must choose to admit the inference or sacrifice credibility. Jurors understand that facts admitted on cross-examination are not self-serving. That is why facts proven on cross are firmer and resonate further than facts proven on direct.

Since Big Facts most strongly compel inferences, a fundamental principle of cross-examination is to keep the questions orbiting around the Big Facts. Following this principle has several benefits. First, if you are focused on Big Facts, then you will ask questions that reveal facts. Second, since Big Facts are central, you will always ask questions about what is relevant and important. In chess terms, you are dominating the center of the board with your most powerful pieces. Third, this approach yields a low-risk, higher-reward area of cross-examination. Asking about Big Facts forces the witness who wants to give you a "bad answer" to dispute a Big Fact or compelling inference. Those kinds of answers are self-inflicted wounds to a witness's credibility. Finally, if you're focused on the Big Facts, it's easier to think on your feet and to ask questions from memory and intuition rather than being chained to notes, which makes for a more powerful and effective cross-examination.

The more Big Facts you incorporate into your case, the more your opponent must explain, dismiss, or attack them, which is the strategic position you want. It puts your opponents on edge, which can lead them to making mistakes on direct examination. A jury will often miss a mistake on direct because the other side wants to pass over it quickly. But mistakes, wrong inferences, and spin about Big Facts are important. Take the time to bring these out on cross-examination. When you need to impeach inaccurate testimony, do it cumulatively, so you can show mistake after mistake in a pattern that will do harm to the witness's credibility.

Indeed, so valuable is the role of Big Facts in determining the outcome of the case, that knowing them and working them to your advantage contributes more to the mastery of cross-examination than your charm or personality. This is because knowing the Big Facts and being comfortable with the inferences that flow from them allows you to relax—you know what will happen next, you're in control. You can afford to be courteous rather than exhibit a false and unctuous charm. Your courtesy gives you an advantage and is a way to coax out good answers.

There is truth at the center of each case. Find the Big Facts and you will be close to the center. Cross-examine using Big Facts and you will find that your cross-examination is effective, efficient, fluid, and true.

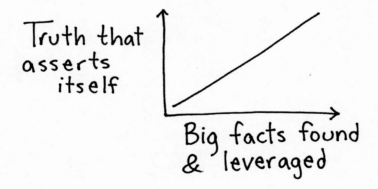

CHAPTER SUMMARY

Main Takeaway

Big Facts win cases. Cases turn on the big, indisputable facts. Make your case and your cross-examination around the Big Facts. They are the truth at the center of the case.

Earthquake Points

- Find the Big Facts in a case and cross-examine on them.

- Big Facts are often not obvious. Taking time to perceive an important fact that others don't see will give you an advantage.

- Big Facts relate to the physical world: guns, clothing, blood, contracts, bills, bank statements.

- A Big Fact creates strong inferences. A fact is only as important as the inferences it creates. Pay attention to lesser facts if they relate directly to Big Facts.

- Avoid cross-examining witnesses on disputed facts. Help the judge and jury by sticking to the undisputed Big Facts, leading them to one inescapable conclusion.

- Keep your questions orbiting around the Big Facts. Use them like powerful chess pieces that dominate the center of the board.

Part 2

THE TRIAL

CHAPTER 4

DEEP PREPARATION

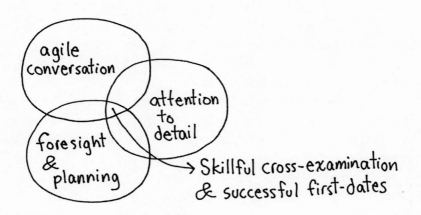

Expect the Unexpected.

—Heracleitus, Greek philosopher

HOW DO YOU PREPARE FOR AN ACTIVITY that requires split-second reactions in a stressful and complex situation? How can you prepare to listen to and digest what the witness has said, understand its implications for your case, and then choose, first, the right topic, and then the right words and manner of presentation for your next question—all while standing alone in front of your adversary, the judge, the jury, and the courtroom spectators?

When you cross-examine, you must—all in an instant—process information; draw on your memory bank of facts; use logic and intuition; perform, control, and elicit emotion; argue; persuade; and improvise. Cross-examination is inquisition, dispute, performance, persuasion, truth seeking, and truth showing, all in one act. You are talking (asking questions) and controlling your tone, volume, and emotion; you are listening (let's hope you are) and taking in information, analyzing it, and making decisions about whether it's important and whether to pursue new information or continue along with your plan. There is a lot going on, even in the simplest cross-examination.

Weinstein writes that cross-examination can "expose inconsistencies, incompleteness, and inaccuracies in the testimony."[1] To those three *i*'s I will add that cross-examination should expose answers that are implausible, improbable, interested, incomprehensible, impossible, and insidious (in the sense of putting forth the "big lie" by repeating talking points). You have to identify how an answer fits one of these adjectives, or some similar logical flaw, and pull up from your working mind a responsive tactic.

In my opinion, the three most difficult skills that a good lawyer must develop are:

1. The ability to summon facts on your feet in order to engage in what appears to be free-flow cross-examination.

2. The ability to smoothly answer pointed, loaded questions posed by an appellate panel of judges.

3. The ability to present an argument or summation in a complex case without notes.

---

[1] Jack B. Weinstein and Margaret A. Berger, *Weinstein's Evidence Manual*, 10th ed., § 14.01 (Durham, NC: Carolina Academic Press, 2015).

These three skills are the mark of trial mastery. They all depend on deep preparation prior to trial. By deep preparation I mean that you must have internalized the case so that you can talk in depth with a command of the facts about any aspect of the case, from any perspective.

The best cross-examination, like summation, is performed without notes. This doesn't mean you don't bring any papers to the podium, but you must have internalized the facts, goals, and forms of questions so that you are doing a minimum of reading and looking at papers. If the thought is not in your mind and available for you to call up in a second, it is of no use to you on cross-examination. In a critical cross-examination—and this is true even at a deposition—you cannot depend on paper or PowerPoint slides unless you have in your mind the information in those documents and can summon it for use without fussing or hunting through a stack of papers.

You must prepare for any activity in a way that is suited for the specific characteristics of the activity. I call cross-examination a "polytropic" activity. That word comes from Homer's description of his hero Odysseus in the *Odyssey*. It means "many turning" or "having many facets or dimensions." So your preparation for cross-examination will be many faceted, to allow you to respond to the multiple and shifting demands of the courtroom, so that like Odysseus, you will be ready for anything.

Why Deep?

By following the advice in the two previous chapters and honing down and weighing your facts, you have already done significant good preparation. But you cannot get to a high level of the skills mentioned above simply by memorizing facts (although a good memory for facts is important). The information you must have in mind includes not only simple facts but also context connections, inferences, implications, and narratives. You are preparing not only your conscious mind, but your intuition and instincts, so that when the witness gives a certain answer the right question comes to mind without conscious thought.

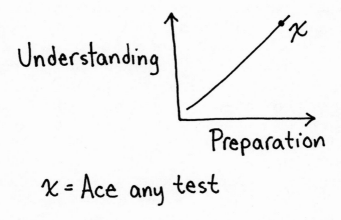

x = Ace any test

Fast and Slow Thinking

How do you prepare your mind to perform in this way? The answer comes from Princeton psychologist Daniel Kahneman, who won the Nobel Memorial Prize in Economics in 2002. Kahneman and his colleague Amos Tversky (who died before he could be awarded the Nobel Prize) created the field of behavioral finance, which is really the study of human thinking, decision making, and judgment. Kahneman's book *Thinking Fast and Slow*[2] comes pretty close to explaining and answer-

---

[2] New York: Farrar, Straus, and Giroux, 2011.

ing the questions I asked myself when I started to write this book: What goes on in my mind when I'm cross-examining? How does the process work?

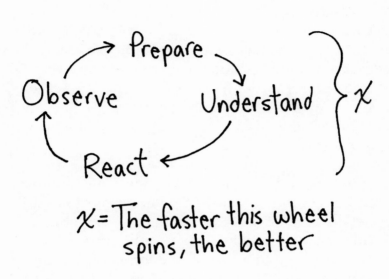

X = The faster this wheel spins, the better

Kahneman describes two systems of thought in the mind. System 1 is fast thinking, which is quick, intuitive, and instinctive—meaning ancient and survival oriented. Fast thinking is sensory and feels like it's happening to you, rather than as if you're doing it. Fast thinking also gives you a premonition of what will happen next, the kind of anticipation that is so essential in survival situations. Although Kahneman doesn't say this, I connect fast thinking with *physical looseness and flexibility*, and with *physical and mental fluidity*, especially among practiced or conscious fast thinkers.

System 2, slow thinking, requires conscious work, effort, and strain. You must draw on your memory to retrieve facts and cognitive programs or methods that you have used to confront similar situations in the past. Slow thinking is deliberate and orderly and is characterized by a feeling of physical strain, a physical tension. It's hard work. Does System 2 sound familiar? That's because it's what lawyers usually think of as thinking, without being aware that there is any other way of thinking.

Cross-examination, at its best, is System 1 thinking. Fast thinking, as I have experienced it, can create, in an exchange of a few seconds, insight and truth that I did not understand through dozens of hours of methodical System 2–style preparation.

Here is what Kahneman says about the two systems as they relate to our subject:

> When we think of ourselves, we identify with System 2, the conscious reasoning self that has beliefs, makes choices, and decides what to think about and what to do. Although System 2 believes itself to be where the action is, the automatic *System 1 is the hero of the book.* I describe System 1 as effortlessly originating impressions and feelings that are the main sources of the explicit beliefs and deliberate choices of System 2. The automatic operations of System 1 generate surprisingly complex patterns of ideas, but only the slower System 2 can construct thoughts in an orderly series of steps. [There are] circumstances in which System 2 takes over, overruling the freewheeling impulses and associations of System 1.[3]

All lawyers know how to prepare in System 2 slow-thinking mode. The problem is that after preparing in this way, we also speak and ask questions as if we were

---

[3] Ibid., 21, emphasis added.

still in the slow thinking mode. But think of Abraham Lincoln. He was a classic deep and slow thinker who would ponder over thoughts and decisions. He worked on a particular speech over a period of months, thinking, revising, making short notes whenever he thought of them and storing the little papers in his hat. Yet when he spoke, he was brief, incisive, and powerful—anything but slow and ponderous. In this chapter I will talk about a number of ways that you can prepare so that your complex System 1 fast-thinking, intuitive, perceptual brain will be prepared and engaged.

An illustration of how slow and fast thinking work together are two books about how the U.S. government found and killed Osama bin Laden. The first book, *The Finish: The Killing of Osama bin Laden*, by Mark Bowden,[4] described the years-long process carried out by intelligence agents. That involved sifting through tens of thousands of pieces of data, some reliable and some not, to try to figure out a theory of where bin Laden might be located—classic analytical slow thinking. What is connected, what is random? What is reliable information, what is not? What is there, what is missing? As an aside, some of the most important facts that intelligence uncovered were "negative facts"—things that should have been there but were missing, the "dog that didn't bark." That the house bin Laden was suspected of hiding in had no phone, no internet, and no outside contact and that at least one person never left the house were critical facts. That Khalid Sheikh Mohammed, the mastermind behind the 9/11 attack and many others, denied under torture that Abu Ahmed was a courier for Bin Laden or was in any way important, when others had identified him as bin Laden's personal courier, was also signifi-

---

[4] New York: *Atlantic Monthly Press*, 2012.

cant. The team engaged in a lot of devil's-advocate critical thinking.

Like a lot of important decisions, all of this information, evaluated with slow thinking, did not lead to certainty about bin Laden's whereabouts, but only probability. In the end, if Bowden's account is correct, President Obama, after hearing the probability estimates from his intelligence executives, pegged the decision to invade bin Laden's compound in Pakistan as having a 50/50 chance of success.

That is what slow thinking gets you: after protracted, deliberate data analysis you get something that may be, but is not certainly, a true story. In this example the story is that bin Laden, the most wanted man in the world, has totally withdrawn from all electronic communication. He communicates only through one highly trusted courier, whom he lives with in a house that is both physically and electronically isolated from the outside world. The courier is a confirmed member of Al-Qaeda. Electronic intelligence gathered by drone reveals that there is a male living on the third floor of the house, but he is never observed physically. There are very few persons who can fit the profile of the electronically and physically concealed man, the most likely —but not certain—being bin Laden.

The process used to capture Osama bin Laden is analogous to the deep thinking preparation that you need to engage in to find the truth at the heart of your case. With this kind of analysis and preparation, you understand your cross-examination goals, which facts you can rely on, which facts are probable, which ones are not. The thinking that found bin Laden's location was classic slow thinking: logical, analytical, based on writings, interviews, and documents.

But now let's look at the second part of the story, as told by Mark Owen, the pseudonymous author of the unauthorized book *No Easy Day: The Firsthand Account of the Mission that Killed Osama bin Laden.*[5] Owen was later revealed to be Matt Bissonnette, a Navy Seal in the United States Naval Special Warfare Development Group. His book tells the fast-thinking part of the story of bin Laden's capture. It is characterized by action, instant decisions, helicopters crashing, and people jumping out of dark doorways or shooting through doors. The Navy SEALs who raided the compound and killed bin Laden prepared for years, before this mission ever existed, as part of their standard training. They prepared first by practicing small specific tasks: shooting, breaking through doors, recognizing friend from foe, moving in the dark with night-vision glasses, rappelling down ropes from helicopters. This is the kind of muscle-memory preparation that allowed them, in an uncertain and chaotic situation, to quickly solve problems that arose unexpectedly. They drew from a toolbox of practiced skills to enhance their chances of success. In fact, not only did they practice the specific skills, they also practiced improvising.

This kind of preparation is visual, tactile, physical, intuitive, instinctive, fluid, improvisational, and skill based. It is preparation for fast thinking. How does this relate to cross-examination? Like the bin Laden operation, success in the courtroom relies on both methodical, multidimensional slow-thinking preparation and fast thinking. To get the best of both modes, you have to be aware of both and understand how they are different. There will come a time when you shift from slow-thinking preparation and prepare to be a fast thinker.

---

[5] New York: New American Library, 2012.

Prepare in Many Dimensions

The best way to prepare for a multidimensional activity is to prepare in many dimensions. Most lawyers don't do this. They simply write out their questions or make an outline. They may spend hours sifting through documents and organizing them late into the night. But if you have only prepared by writing questions and an outline, you will be speechless when the witness deviates from your plan. This kind of preparation is stiff, structured, and limited, when you want to be *fluid, agile, relaxed,* and *open.* The witness will always deviate from your plan, so you must plan for the unexpected.

That's why you can't just prepare for the cross-examination of a witness in isolation. Every fact, every witness is part of the larger tapestry, and if you can't see and understand the whole case in its many facets, you will not be at your best in cross-examination.

The dimensions of preparation involve many different ways of conceptualizing, organizing, questioning, and reconsidering information from many points of view, using a variety of practical strategies, and engaging your mind and body in a variety of ways, including physical movement, your senses, your emotions, and your imagination. In multidimensional preparation you are working with the case facts, with all aspects of yourself (intellectual, emotional, physical), and with your opponent in as many ways as possible.

To prepare in many dimensions means that you not only sit down and write out a list of points you want to make on cross-examination of a witness, but you also prepare your mind for the many ways that the exchange between you and the witness may play out. Cross-examination is not done on paper by writing and answering questions back and forth, so preparing in that way is just the start. I find that to be good news, since you can accomplish a lot without drudgery.

As you prepare, don't forget to use your body as well as your mind. Walk and talk. Find someone to act as the witness and have a back-and-forth conversation with the person. Even standing up alone in an empty room and asking your question in a number of different ways creates surprising new dimensions for understanding the question. One hour spent doing this is more effective than many hours spent at a desk. As I will discuss in chapter 9, physical action engages thinking in a number of ways, and the simple act of getting up out of your chair will almost always produce at least one good thought that you would not have had by simply sitting and reading the case documents.

Those are some specific examples of multi-dimensional preparation, but you will find others. Information enters your mind through different senses and dimensions. Rather than having to remember a list of points, you might recall a fact by its visual relationship with another fact, or recall words or phrases to use in cross-examination because you remember their sound.

Take a Broader View to See Relationships Among Parts

Linear preparation is the conventional way that lawyers begin preparing for cross-examination. You start by writing out a line of questions that you want to ask a witness as they come to your mind. This line is either chronological or logical in that it leads straight to the point you want to make.

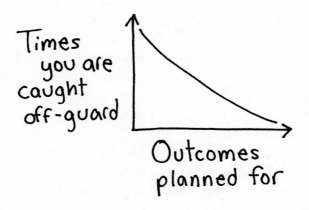

A limitation of this method is that it keeps you focused on the individual details of your case and you can forget how each detail fits into the whole picture. Sometimes this can take you down a path that diverges more and more from your main goals.

You can enhance your linear preparation by taking an overview and seeing the relationship of the parts to the whole. Take a big step back from the details of your case and begin by listing the goals and points that you want to make in the *entire* case. Make a list of the facts in the case, both "good" and "bad," that you are most certain are true. Next think about the relationship of each smaller goal to the big case goals.

This whole-to-part approach can be applied to

many different aspects of case preparation. You can discover the specific goals for each witness from this overview. You can use it to make lists of facts and exhibits, as well as topics that fit together and then into a whole. You can make a chronology and see how time relates to the facts and topics you have already organized.

This approach leads to a deeper, more intuitive understanding of the dimensions of your case. You're thinking about how this witness fits into the case as a whole and how your goals for each witness relate to the other evidence and to the whole. When you look at the questions and evidence from these different angles, your mind internalizes them more easily so that you will be able to recall them and use them when you need to.

The overview approach will help you organize your case facts and materials in your mind. Looking for facts and documents is the biggest loss of time, not only for lawyers but for all knowledge workers. In the courtroom it will confuse and distract you. Organize or die!

You should have all the facts in one place, no matter what their source. Organize them first by goal, then by topic, then chronologically. In organizing your documents, keep all like things in one place. All documents related to one witness, meeting, important person, related data, and so on should be in the same file. This may mean filing duplicate copies of a document if it relates to more than one thing. For example, a medical report might relate to a specific witness, a hearing, and a deposition and could be filed in each of those folders. This will help you not only to find the document when you need it, but also to see how facts relate to a number of different aspects of the case.

I am not going into great depth on the organizational aspect of preparation, because it is natural to lawyers. It is the traditional analytical way of preparing a case. My suggestion is that you approach your case in a broader, more connected way so that you're certain of how each detail fits into the larger picture of the overall case goals.

Reverse Preparation

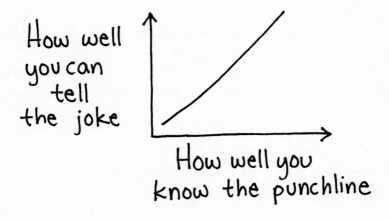

Once you have your linear preparation in place, the best way to prepare is to do everything in reverse, by putting the last things first. The Greeks called this technique "hysteron proteron," which means "putting the other thing first." The very last words that the jury will hear before deliberation are the judge's charge. Few lawyers think about the charge before trial. But the charge is what the jury will use to process information about the case. Facts that answer questions in the jury charge are the biggest, most important facts in the case. Use them prominently in your cross-examination.

Since your summation or closing argument is the last words you will say to the jury just before the charge, you should write out your final argument using all of your "atoms"—those unadorned facts that you have found to be real and true. In your argument you will retell the story that is at the heart of your case. This is a working story, not a final story, but by writing it out, with a beginning, middle, and end, you will be amazed at how much you learn.

Once it is written out, then you proceed in reverse. You go step by step back to the atoms that you have spent time thinking about and that got somehow embellished and combined when you wrote out your story in narrative form. Some bias and self-serving distortion may have crept in. Now you outline your story and study it objectively, taking out all arguments and inferences until you have an organized outline of factual statements. Then compress the outline further, to a small list that fits on one page. Be conscious of the language you use: compress vague or lawyer terms into sharp, vivid, concrete words. Then compress further, until the bare bones of your story can fit onto a small index card. You can even use Post-it notes to reflect the separateness and smallness of the facts that you have extracted from your narrative, as well as the moveability of facts from one part of a narrative to another. These notes, affixed to your case documents, remind you of the essentials and encourage you to use short, sharp questions in cross-examination.

Reverse preparation is related to taking a broader view of your case. It keeps you on track to where your case should be going and strengthens your mental grasp on the case. It helps you understand how the parts of your case relate to the whole. This gives you further insights into different angles or perspectives that straightforward linear preparation may not yield. Reverse preparation forces you to distill your story to its essence, boiling it down to its bare bones. Later you will build it back up again, from simple facts back into a story, and it will probably be somewhat different from your original narrative.

Visual Preparation

Trial strategy is often described as a puzzle or a mosaic, in which you take small pieces of various shapes and colors and fit them together into a whole to make a larger picture. When the tiles of the mosaic or the pieces of the puzzle are in disarray on the floor, what do you do? You put like colors together, you chunk together smaller parts that fit together, *all the while looking back and forth from the big picture on the puzzle box to the pieces that lie before you*. You make small structures of facts that explain one another and explain an important part of the story. You try to understand how these facts fit together with each other and where they fit into the story.

When you prepare in this way, the facts, issues, and relationships of the case sink deeply into your mind in a natural way that allows you to quickly summon related facts and to ask questions based on relationships. It becomes as easy for your mind to quickly call up a group of related facts as one isolated or out of context fact. This is a far more powerful method of preparing than making lists because it is more in tune with the story process that your mind naturally uses to organize complex information. Your mind also becomes intuitive about what fits and what doesn't fit your picture of the case, so that if the witness says something off the wall, your mind can immediately recognize and seize on it.

Many lawyers understand this mosaic or pixel concept, and yet they still prepare by writing outlines and questions. A better way to prepare is to create a picture of your case by organizing the points or information visually, not in a list. By drawing a mind map you engage both your visual brain and your brain-to-hand dimension of thinking. This lets you see facts not only in chronology, but by topic and relationship all at once in a way a list does not. If you prepare in this way, the right information will come to your conscious mind easily during cross-examination, rather than having to search for it by going down a mental checklist.

Draw fact maps that show how facts and people fit together. Organize the facts in circles, varying the size of the circle to depict relative weight or importance of facts, and use colors to indicate whether and how much a fact is in dispute. Link the circles with motivations and causes and effects.

One way to view your case visually is as a solar system, with the most influential and significant facts at the center. Draw circles around them, again using the size of the circle to show the importance of the facts. More important facts will influence or compel the logic of smaller facts. Also draw your adversary's case from the perspective of its most important and influential facts.

On the following page is a simple mind map based on one I actually used to prepare to cross-examine the CEO of a large health insurance company. (I have removed or changed anything that could identify the company or executives.)

The company undertook a massive overhaul of its computer systems. The CEO told investors at press conferences and in SEC filings that the conversion was going well and that there were no problems. Some investigative securities analysts learned that there was a large backlog of unprocessed patient claims and many complaints from healthcare providers who had submitted claims to be paid. At a press conference the CEO made the false statement in the center oval, that

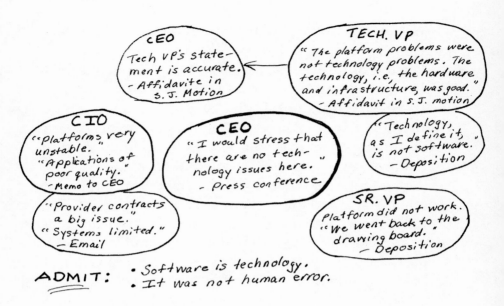

CEO
Tech VP's statement is accurate.
- Affidavite in S. J. Motion

TECH. VP
" The platform problems were not technology problems. The technology, i.e, the hardware and infrastructure, was good."
- Affidavit in s.J. motion

CIO
"platforms" very unstable.
"Applications of poor quality."
- Memo to CEO

CEO
" I would stress that there are no technology issues here. "
- Press conference

"Technology, as I define it, is not software."
- Deposition

"Provider contracts a big issue."
" Systems limited."
- Email

SR. VP
Platform did not work.
"We went back to the drawing board."
- Deposition

ADMIT:
- Software is technology.
- It was not human error.

there were "no technology issues" and that the delays were due to human errors and not the computer systems conversion. Investors sued the company and the CEO for making false and misleading statements in violation of securities laws. The two ovals on the left show internal messages that the CEO received that contradicted his public statements, revealing his awareness of the problem. The ovals at the top and on the right show the executives' sworn statements. At summary judgment, a technology senior vice-president swore in an affidavit that there were no technology issues, attempting to limit the definition of technology to "hardware and infrastructure." Of course the technology at issue was software and the goal of the cross-examination was to get the CEO to admit that, thus contradicting his public statement to investors. The mind map allowed me to diagram seven statements at the heart of this complex case to arrive at a simple statement of the two admissions I needed to achieve in cross-examination. Here you have on one sheet of paper a visual image condensed from many large files, in a way that the mind can easily grasp.

Play with these drawings. Move facts, people, events, and questions around. Redraw sizes and relationships. As you do this, as with linear relational preparation, the facts are sinking into your brain in a way that is far more memorable and useful than making lists or outlines of them. But also new contexts and connections will come up from your subconscious.

Another type of visual preparation is to draw the case as a general draws the map of a battle. Instead of drawing a vertical line down the center of your page and putting good and bad facts on either side as you've been taught, turn the paper horizontally and draw a line across it. Draw icons representing the most important facts on either side. Draw the adversary's counterfacts and arguments directly across from your facts that they address. Draw your counterfacts across from your adversary's. Try drawing (or at least visualizing) the battle as a chessboard, with some facts as powerful pieces and others as pawns.

Are there facts on either side that are not countered? Are some facts supported and made stronger by others? If so, put them together as you would supporting elements in a battle plan. Stand up and look at the battle map from above to get a different view. You might get ideas on how to flank your adversary's facts and arguments. You will certainly have a better grasp of what facts to call up from reserves when a witness gives you an answer containing one of the other side's good facts.

Multisensory Rehearsal

There are other lessons that lawyers can learn from soldiers, firefighters, and others who must prepare to act in a rapidly changing scenario. In one of my favorite childhood movies, *The Dirty Dozen*, Major Reisman, played by Lee Marvin, is assigned the job of preparing his uneducated, unmotivated, and unruly unit for a complex and dangerous raid on a French chateau that is heavily guarded by the Nazis. He uses two methods. First he creates a childish-sounding rhyme that sets out in simple terms what needs to be done, by whom, and in what order. The rhyme has few details and doesn't say how the soldiers are supposed to obtain the desired results. Then he makes a three-dimensional mock-up with a model of the hotel and toy soldiers, vehicles, and weapons. The major demonstrates the mission and lets the soldiers play it out with their little toy soldiers. The hardened-criminal soldiers giggle happily as they move the toy soldiers and recite the rhyme.

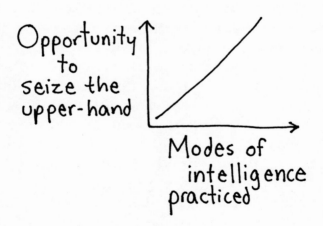

The major has hit on the best way to learn a complex activity that requires thinking through time and space. He is using multisensory learning. He engages the musical part of his men's brains with the singsong rhyme.

Music is an art that moves through time. He engages the visual, tactile, and motor intelligences of his soldiers by having them move the toy soldiers through the planned raid. And he does everything simultaneously, engaging the musical, verbal, spatial, tactile, and visual intelligences all at once. This is the most efficient way to learn a plan that will have to be carried out at a fast pace under stress and in physical danger.

Prepare Like an Actor

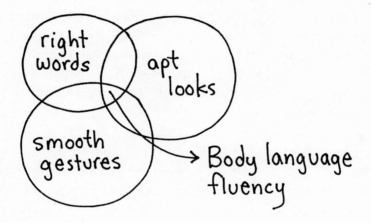

In law school there are no courses in how to speak in public, or how to prepare for your moot court trial. Trial-advocacy courses give only brief tips on public speaking and cross-examination.

The key to a good courtroom presentation is to understand that it is not only a verbal activity, but also a performance that you do with your entire person. Lawyers' preparation is generally verbal only. When I was a younger lawyer, the idea of getting up in front of a mirror and practicing my summation occasionally occurred to me, but I didn't do it, nor was I taught to treat it as standard preparation. But if your only preparation is silently reading over documents and papers and writing out your questions, it may take you a long time to develop the instinct to give a relaxed and confident performance. This is a skill that can be learned and practiced until it comes naturally. The key is to prepare in the same way that the activity will happen.

Practice like an actor, asking your questions while standing in front of a mirror or simply standing anywhere. Get the feel of your body as you ask questions. Notice your posture and relax your shoulders. Practice using your hands to gesture. Practice saying the specific words you have listed as facts in your case. At first, the questions will come out long and wordy. Ask them again out loud, this time making them shorter and clearer and putting emphasis on the proper words. Practice "punching" the most important words. You will notice that shorter, clearer words also have more emotional impact.

Now, while standing alone in the middle of the room, imagine a witness giving an answer that shocks or upsets you. This kind of answer is usually a lie, distortion, or exaggeration that is clever and unexpected. You have not prepared for it. It puts you under emotional stress. You're standing there exposed. How do you react? How do you remain calm and continue thinking clearly? Lawyers lose their composure when they're surprised by something that goes outside their prepared plan. If you have thought in advance about how you will deal with this type of answer, you won't be surprised by anything. Prepare for the worst case as described below and rehearse your response to a witness's most damaging statement.

If you rehearse like an actor, standing up and visualizing yourself in the courtroom, you will be amazed at the improvement in your cross-examination perfor-mance in the rapid give-and-take of the moment.

Simplicity Is Key

Returning to *The Dirty Dozen*, a key point in Major Reisman's training regimen was simplicity. The rhyme he devised for his troops was simply, "One two, the guards are through," rather than "Sneak up behind the guards, one man to the left and one to the right, your bayonets ready, and when I give you the signal, jump into position and attack."

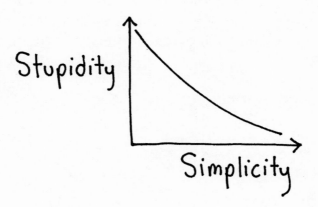

The major's soldiers may have been unusually inept, but in fact simplicity is essential for everyone preparing for a stressful activity. When under stress, the human brain cannot engage in complex techniques and can-not remember anything complicated. Stress forces the brain into fight-or-flight mode, which causes some of the higher cognitive functions to shut down. If you have to remember anything complicated, like a process that requires several steps, you won't be able to do it.

You won't remember the numerous steps for impeaching testimony with an inconsistent statement when you stand up, the jury is looking at you expectantly, and the judge is saying, "Move on, Counsel. Are you finished?"

This is why the final stage of your preparation for cross-examination should include reviewing your case and removing everything that isn't essential, focusing on your main goals and the main facts, documents, and cross-examination questions that lead to those goals. Resist the temptation to constantly refine your case by adding to it, like an artist who is always touching up a painting that's never finished. Do the opposite and continually cut the nonessentials to sharpen your focus and reduce the case to what you can reasonably hold in your mind under stress. As you do that you will simplify things for the judge and jury as well. We will look at specific ways of achieving simplicity in chapter 5.

Metapreparation

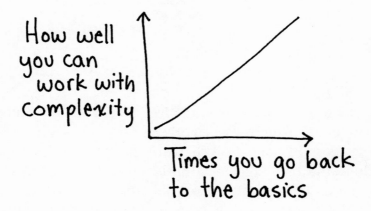

Metapreparation means returning, after you have immersed yourself in the facts, inferences, probabilities, and possibilities of your case, to the basic principles of cross-examination, argument, and persuasion. These are often simple, almost obvious basics that you learned in law school or at the beginning of your career. Returning again and again to these fundamental ideas and incorporating them into your case will distinguish you from the majority of lawyers. *Mastery is mastery of the basics.* Experienced lawyers can learn something new by remembering something they have read many times, now applied to a new case.

After you've amassed the facts, go back to the story to help you better form the questions that you will ask witnesses. In the same way that simplicity is an important overarching principle in the preparation of your case, you should return to other important principles of persuasion and understand how your case fits with them and how you can improve your planned cross-examination by applying these principles to your facts. I know that in preparing for trial you have a million things to do, but metapreparation can give you the edge that makes the difference between a sharp, well-presented case and one that just misses the mark.

For example, you can consider whether your cross-examination fits into classical principles of persuasive speaking. Most trial lawyers have a library of books about trial practice. Mine starts with *The Rhetoric* by Aristotle, in which he sets out the three principles of persuasive speech: ethos (your credibility), pathos (appealing to the intuition, instinct, and emotions of the judge and jury), and logos (logical reasoning). When I'm planning a cross-examination, after I have ingested and know the case and am trying to make choices about what is key, what should come first, and how it should end, I might reread the section of *The Rhetoric* that discusses these principles and then get the insight that if I have only one topic to cross-examine about, it will be to impeach the character of the main witness, and that I should save my arguments about the case's logical flaws for summation. It is not a waste of time to read something not directly related to the case. In fact it will often become the source of a creative outside-the-box insight that could help your case. I hope you might use this book in that way.

Doing this metapreparation helps you shape your facts at an early stage into the forms that are most effective, as discovered and written about by masters of the art of persuasion. At this stage I often also reread Irving Younger's Ten Commandments of Cross-Examination. I once had them printed on the back of my business cards and laminated so I could carry them in my wallet.

Most lawyers learn the basics of cross-examination, and because they are the basics, assume they are easy and once learned, they will be held forever in the mind. But in fact you need to continually return to these basics and measure your preparation against them. For example, you probably know that the first rule of cross-examination is "Ask short, simple questions." But it takes discipline to counteract our natural tendency to ask complicated questions about a complex case. If you reread Younger's Ten Commandments as you go over the facts and documents in your case, you will almost always think of ways to ask better questions.

Each time you return again to one of the basic principles in a new case, you will bring with you, first, the unique application of the principle to the case, and second, all you have learned on your previous visits to the principle. By doing this you will gain a much deeper understanding and mastery of the principle. I call this the spiral of mastery. The principles of cross-examination can be visualized in a circle, and each time you review them in your metapreparation, you understand them at the next higher level, like walking up a spiral staircase. I will discuss this idea more in chapter 10, on learning and mastery.

Metapreparation is like the fast-thinking preparation of Navy SEALs. Just as the SEALs practice breaking open doors, shooting while moving, and a number of other actions that form the basics of their craft that they apply again and again to a variety of different missions, you will master cross-examination by returning to the basic elements of questioning and persuasive thinking, and then applying those principles to each new case in a unique way.

I consider the review of these basic principles as a standard element of a well-prepared case, just as important, for example, as a physical visit to the crime scene is in a criminal case.

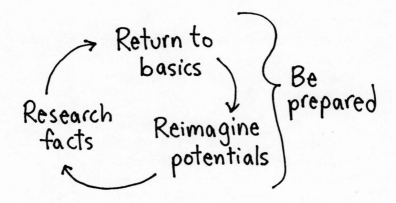

CHAPTER SUMMARY

Main Takeaway

Deep preparation means assembling your facts, working through the connections among them, and constructing them into narratives. It means viewing the facts from many different angles and working with them in many different ways so that the case becomes part of you. Thus prepared, you can cross-examine fluidly without notes in a constantly changing and complex trial environment.

Earthquake Points

- For rapid insights and reactions during cross-examination you need intuitive fast thinking. Preparation for fast thinking is visual, physical, fluid, improvisational, and skill based.

- Don't just write out questions and an outline. Prepare in many dimensions: Engage your mind and body in many different ways. Practice with someone playing the role of the witness. Get up, walk around, think out loud.

- Take a panoramic overview of your case and see the relationship of the parts to the whole.

- Visual thinking gives insight into complex things. Prepare visually using mind maps to organize your facts, points, and people and see the relationships among them. Do the same for your opponent's case.

- Practice fast thinking skills as well as slow.

- Prepare like an actor: stand in front of a mirror and ask your questions. Rehearse your response to unexpected and worst-case answers.

- Use reverse preparation: start with your final argument, then work backwards to understand how to bring out the evidence you will need in your summation.

- Be guided by the basic principle of getting to the clear and simple truth at the heart of your case.

- As you are preparing the specific facts of your case, also review the fundamental principles of cross-examination, like Aristotle's principles of persuasion and Younger's Ten Commandments.

CHAPTER 5

SIMPLICITY

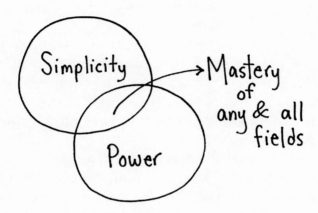

In Jeet Kune Do, one does not accumulate, but eliminate. It is not daily increase, but daily decrease. The height of cultivation always runs to simplicity. Before I studied the art, a punch to me was just like a punch, a kick just like a kick. After I learned the art, a punch was no longer a punch, a kick no longer a kick. Now that I've understood the art, a punch is just like a punch, a kick just like a kick. The height of cultivation is really nothing special. It is merely simplicity; *the ability to express the utmost with the minimum*. It is the halfway cultivation that leads to ornamentation. Jeet Kune Do is basically a sophisticated fighting style stripped to its essentials.

—Bruce Lee, *Tao of Jeet Kune Do* (emphasis added)

"THE ABILITY TO EXPRESS THE UTMOST with the minimum." I can think of no better way to express the essence of good lawyering. This chapter will help you understand what true simplicity is in cross-examination and will offer you strategies for mastering the art of simplicity in order to *stay close to the heart of your case* and *keep the judge and jury focused on your central truth* as well.

The insight that Bruce Lee expresses above is that beginners often have a false understanding of an art as simple. They oversimplify. A true understanding of simplicity comes only after the long study and work of removing all that is not essential. That kind of punch is simple and powerful.

Simplicity frees the intuition and allows true insight to arise. Clear away the clutter in your case and you will be amazed at what you see. But simplicity in cross-examination does not only benefit lawyers, it benefits judges and juries as well. Lawyers who have been living and learning a case for months and often years underestimate how hard it is for juries and even judges to understand the case when they hear it for the first time. Cross-examination that is not only simple, but connected to a theme that is also unified and simple, will be easier to understand and more effective.

Most lawyers hate simplicity. Therefore simplicity is the way to have the competitive advantage over lawyers who hold fast to the belief that "more is better." Although lawyers are drawn to complexity like a moth to a flame, simplicity fits the natural tendencies and abilities of the human mind much better, including the minds of lawyers and judges and juries. Since the human mind cannot hold too many things in focus at once, you can achieve simplicity by putting all of your effort and power into one simple theme or story, and then connecting all the details and facts to that center of your case. Follow the model of a fighter who puts all of his body and all his power, from the base of his feet up through his legs, torso, chest, shoulders, arms, and fists, into the punch, rather than the fighter who is throwing many loopy, disconnected punches.

Work to Find Simplicity

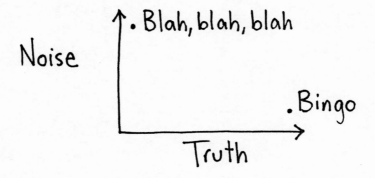

True simplicity is not easy; it's hard. It must strike at the heart of the matter in a way that is true. The above quote from martial artist Bruce Lee shows that true simplicity is not immediately visible on the surface. It is only discovered through a continual process of synthesis and stripping away, a process that requires the discipline of a martial artist to avoid the temptation of adding more and more to your case.

Even a small case can have hundreds of facts. Without the discipline of simplicity, things rapidly spiral out of control. When you're bogged down in hundreds of documents, you don't have a chance to let your mind play creatively with the facts of the case. Your mind is struggling to simply grasp the facts rather than to penetrate them deeply. You need the discipline of simplicity to go deep, to the true center of your case. If you're going wide, trying to include as much as possible, you won't be able to go deep. The saying "an inch wide, a mile deep" should express your goal.

Simplicity Is the Essence of Your Case

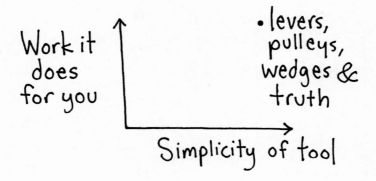

By simplicity, I mean more than an easy, superficial way of looking at things. That's one kind of simplicity, but there is a truer, deeper simplicity that comes from understanding the essence of a case. The simplicity in the essence of a case comes only after understanding all the details, the context, and the way it all fits together. When you have worked through all that, you can come out on the other side with the kind of essential simplicity that unlocks the connections of a case and becomes a simple and powerful way of understanding and explaining everything in the case.

Simplicity is the unifying principle of all aspects of a case: your preparation, discovery documents, case theory, goals, pleadings, and cross-examination questions should all be planned and executed in the simplest way possible. *Seeking the simplest path that does the most work* is the essence of effective cross-examination. Simplicity speaks best, persuades best, is most dramatic, and is the mark of the master. The most powerful facts, narratives, documents, and questions are simple.

Simplicity is a key element in the lawyer's great spiral of Mastery. Simplicity unifies cross-examination with other arts that demand long years of practice and attention—music, painting, and writing, as well as physical arts such as martial arts, archery, and so on—because in all of these disciplines, when you seek simplicity you reveal more and more of the underlying truth that you seek.

There is no course in simplicity in law school, but a daily practice of simplicity will do more to increase your raw legal and trial talent than studying a hundred Supreme Court opinions or learning every regulation of the Securities and Exchange Commission. You will have the chance in any law practice to hear a complicated and knotty story or explanation every day. If you make a practice of seeking to understand its simple whole, you will gain a highly valuable thinking skill. Simplicity is the way to strengthen your legal tendons, the parts that can really do the work with a minimum of muscle, rather than building legal muscle, which is what most of us were taught to do in law school and still try to do.

Admiral Bill McRaven, in his book on successful special operations military missions,[1] writes that simplicity is an essential element of successful military operations. According to McRaven, simplicity has three elements:

- *Limited objectives.* You can't try to do too many things in a complex, dynamic situation.

---

[1] *Spec Ops: Case Studies in Special Operations Warfare, Theory and Practice* (New York: Presidio, 1996).

- *Intelligence.* You must know in advance the facts that you will be facing on the ground. In the courtroom, this means that your preparation has taken you to the simple heart of your case.

- *Innovation.* You must have a creative strategy. Simple is not conventional.

You will find those three elements of simplicity equally useful for preparing and presenting your case.

Benefits of Simplicity

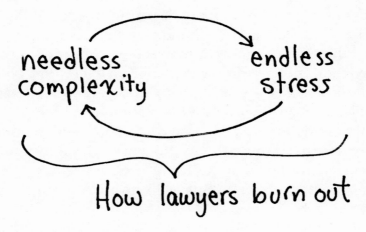

needless complexity → endless stress

How lawyers burn out

Simplicity frees your intuition

If you have fewer choices you can think more clearly. Concentrating on the essence and the central idea of your case lets you go deep into an issue. If you can put aside everything but the most important facts, and relax and concentrate on them, then your instinct for what is really important in the case will develop. You will be able to see the unseen forces, whether human motivations or other deep causes and connections in the case. You can't develop this instinct when you're worrying about how to organize fifty exhibits and carrying two boxes instead of one thin folder into the courtroom. You must give up complexity in order to free your mind. If you actively pursue simplicity from the first day of your case, you will build your instinct for the lucid, pithy, target-striking questions that a good cross-examiner asks.

Simplicity brings clarity

When you limit the number of questions that you need to ask, you can use those few central questions to get deeper into the center of the case. You engage creativity and deep thinking when you put the demand of simplicity on your trial and deposition decisions. You can make your questions work creatively.

Simplicity is the method by which you both seek and communicate knowledge, sharpening your focus as you work through the case during preparing and in the courtroom. It is the key to both reasoning and persuasion. When you're learning your case, gathering information in the form of facts, viewpoints, opinions, and perceptions that may be right or wrong, you're looking for a unifying theory. This is what we learn in law school. But we don't learn when or where to stop. I have been in many cases where plaintiffs' lawyers have kept asking for more and more documents, wanting thousands of papers to sift through, thinking that the more they get, the more likely they will find what they're looking for. What they find instead is that they spend more mental energy organizing paperwork and marshaling documents than they do grappling with the essence of the case. As these documents pile up, the truth of the case becomes obscured under layers of unimportant information.

Simplicity gives you a chance to think. Lawyers love to work long hours, count them up, produce written work to prove that they really were working during all the hours that they billed, and to fill up all available time. The conventional thinking goes that the more exhibits you use at a trial or deposi-tion, the harder you've worked and the better lawyer you are. You need to fight against this norm, because it will prevent you from gaining a deep understanding of your case.

I take great pleasure in walking into the deposition of a CEO with a one-inch binder that comprises all of my documents. When I do that I can look that CEO in the eye and he or she knows I am their equal, and not a document-obsessed and paper-focused functionary. The CEO also knows that whatever is in my thin folder must be very significant, that I have not lost the truth of the case in its complexity, as perhaps the CEO is hoping. You can spend a lot more time being aware if you're not worrying about all the documents you have to cover, and you will be better able to ask intuitive questions if you don't have the false crutch of documents sitting in a big pile in front of you.

Simplicity and comfort with the few rather than the many allow you to perceive the space in between facts, where the real truth often lies. This is clarity.

Simplicity enables fluidity

A legal case possesses a type of energy of its own and in the best-case scenario you want your case to flow smoothly, with no friction or blockages in gathering evidence, finding witnesses, conducting your cross-examination, and so on. And you certainly don't want to fall prey to blockages in your thinking, or even your physical energy. Choosing simplicity in all aspects of your work as a lawyer is key to facilitating the smooth, unimpeded flow of your cases.

In cross-examination fluidity means a smooth, easy movement from fact to fact and from question to question. Most important is ease of movement from a witness's answer to your next question. If you have achieved simplicity you hold in your mind all the information you need to allow your questions to flow. This is because an important aspect of simplicity is that one theme or cluster of facts connects to many others. From the center of simplicity you can quickly and easily intuit how everything fits together, allowing your mind to create the next questions fluidly and easily. Think about the design of a brain cell. It has one central structure with a web of surrounding neurons connecting to and communicating with other cells.

Cases in which there is a huge amount of information, usually documents, are a challenge to simplicity. Most lawyers who have tried such cases will tell you that *the heart of the case generally is decided by the information in ten documents or fewer*. The problem is knowing which ten will be the most important by the end of the trial. So there is a strong urge to keep as many options open as possible. But this builds friction in thinking, and in the progress of the trial and the case. In complex cases with a lot of issues and evidence, you must continually simplify by defining and restating the unifying principle, the big picture, and how each piece of evidence connects to your unifying theme. Your cross-examination should reflect this goal of unity and simplicity. The jury will thank you for being the lawyer who gave them clarity. Most trials involving volumes of documents descend into drudgery.

The physical burden of copying and scanning documents is an obstacle to clear thinking. The more you try to cover, the more topics and questions you have, and the more documents and exhibits you will need. This means more to remember that is not at the core of the case. Trying to remember where fifty documents are—even on a laptop—fills up valuable memory space. It also increases the time, effort, and stress spent on physical logistics, which everyone underestimates as a factor, especially in complex trials.

Do the opposite: pare the facts, your documents, your strategy, and your cross-examination questions down to the minimum to allow your courtroom presentation to flow easily to the central truth of your case, leading the judge and jury smoothly to that truth.

What Is a Simple Cross-Examination?

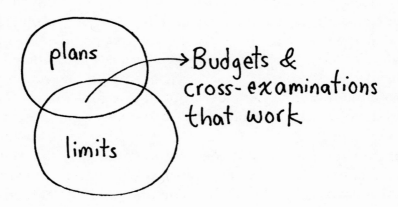

A simple cross-examination is one that is well planned, limited in topics, and structured to the story.

Well planned means that you have organized and command all related facts. Planning means not only preparing for what you intend to do, but also for what can go wrong, and what to do if the witness tries to move you off track. The meaning, the context of the cross-examination can be made in the cross-examination itself, or not.

Limited in topics means giving up a number of points you wish you could make in favor of making only the most important points that are likely to influence the judge and jury. Even if you have ten great topics that you think you can destroy the witness with, by the time you reach the fourth, you will not only lose impact but possibly confuse the jury and even lose your own focus.

The limited list of topics must be integral to the story. Each question is small and sharp, like the whole of the cross-examination. But if your process is right, if you're on the central issue of the case and asking short, sharp questions under control and according to a well-thought-out plan, you dramatically increase your odds of asking that perfect question. You will have understood and asked questions about the facts connecting to the central point of the case. Simplicity is the power, the path that gets you to the perfect question.

Structured to the story means that you ask simple questions that may not seem to be connected but that build your context and story witness by witness. These questions may appear to the witness to be innocuous and unconnected to a narrative or explanation. They are not dramatic and do not catch the witness in a lie or other misrepresentation. Later, with another witness, with other evidence, or in your final argument, you connect these facts and their impact becomes clear. If you're not simple and discreet, the witness will figure out your strategy and fight you. Returning to the metaphor of cross-examination as a mosaic, you ask each witness about one color of tile, and then in your summation, create a full picture with all the different colored tiles you have gathered. No witness has given you a complete picture, but each has given you the means to make one yourself.

The jury is out and has been deliberating for hours or days, enough time for them to have gone through the evidence and to be ready to give their verdict. A note comes out. You never know if it's a question from one holdout or from a majority trying to persuade the holdouts. It usually comes down to some simple question, sometimes a part of the judge's instructions, such as a definition or explanation. Often the jurors ask to have one small part of the questioning of one witness read back. You hear your questions and often think, "Were those questions clear enough? I wish I had asked another question, or asked the question differently, or pinned that answer down with a follow-up question." Listening to such questions from jurors a hundred times with a tight ball in my stomach has made me, at the beginning of the case, try to imagine what that last jury question, the one that tips the last holdouts to a verdict, could be.

An ideal cross-examination has asked that precise question. The question probably didn't cause gasps from the gallery, or cause the witness to break down and cry or admit the crime. You may never really know what the most important question on cross-examination is until the jury sends out a note asking for the testimony of a witness on a particular subject that they consider crucial. If you have stuck to your process, your method of asking short, clear questions that seek the simple essence of the case with each witness, you greatly increase your chances of doing a great cross-examination on the most important topics.

Truth and Simplicity

In chapter 1 we saw that truth is the goal of our legal system and that truth lies at the center of every legal case. There are a lot of distracting facts, and even many compelling facts that don't go to the essence of the thing.

But if you can somehow find that simple unifying truth, you will hold the leverage. You will have the power to quickly understand the flaws in adverse testimony and ask the right question to expose those flaws, rather than freezing and shuffling through your papers as you try to figure out the next question to ask. You will be able to instantly get to the point, which in the English language means something small and sharp.

Lawyers can and do win cases by oversimplifying, using charisma and the principles of propaganda. A false simplicity, charismatically presented, can defeat a complicated truth. At some time in your career you will come up against highly skilled false simplicity. If you want to defeat it you will need the skill of true simplicity.

Techniques of Simplicity

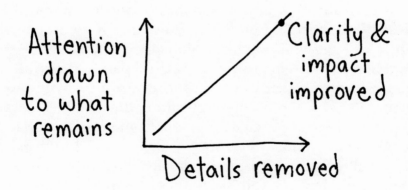

Decide whether to cross-examine a witness at all

Less is better, and often if the witness has not hurt you, and you cannot develop a significant positive fact from that witness, the best strategy is to not cross-examine. But if the witness has testified in a way that is harmful to your case you must determine if cross-examination is the best way to refute the witness. You could use other evidence or other witnesses. However, if a witness has hurt your case, it is better to at least set up the contradicting evidence or witnesses with a few questions, rather than completely forgo cross-examination.

In the age of video-taped depositions in almost all civil cases, this is really the very best option. You simply set up the witness to make the statement that contradicts prior testimony—of course it must be an important witness and an important topic—and then you're done. You play the contradicting testimony on summation.

Have the courage to destroy information

In his book on computer intelligence, inventor and computer scientist Ray Kurzweil writes, "Intelligence is precisely the process of selecting relevant information carefully so that it can skillfully and purposefully destroy the rest."[2] Simplicity is about what you leave out. As Kurzweil suggests, nonaction, silence, doing nothing, and leaving things out are all part of the strategic and tactical creative process. They are also an underestimated aspect of high practical intelligence.

Removing as much as possible from your case challenges your mind to find the most important information that remains. Information means data, facts, atoms, events, evidence, exhibits, witnesses, and arguments. Hack away at all of these, removing as many as possible until you're working the vein of the case. Leave aside the merely important and focus on what is essential.

---

[2] *The Age of Spiritual Machines: When Computers Exceed Human Intelligence* (New York: Penguin, 2000).

Eliminate your second-best hand

Simplicity is the practice, the discipline of staying on the most important thing and not being distracted by petty points that make you look good or bad. You can also be distracted by significant points that are not of number one importance. Trials often become about one single fact, one single event, one single question, whether answered or not. There can be a lot of back-and-forth by lawyers exploring all angles through all witnesses on this one point. So when you're choosing the topics of your cross-examination, you should be able to draw a clear line from each point back to the central topic of your case.

A very common way to lose big money in poker is to have the second-best hand. That means you have a really good hand, perhaps three kings, and you can't conceive of anyone having a better hand so you make a big bet. After all, three kings is the best hand you've been dealt all night. Of course you're shocked when your adversary has three aces and you lose your pile.

For cross-examination, every word you spend on your second-best point is a loss. It's a high-risk bet on something that you can lose big on.

You must eliminate and destroy less important points on cross-examination. By less important I mean points that are not directly connected to your main purpose. This means that *the excellence of your cross-examination is determined more by what you leave out than what you put in*. You cannot expect to land the master stroke if you don't concentrate your attention, your effort, and your purpose on the most important point, the most important goal. My best examinations have been when I have said to my colleagues beforehand, "This is the one and only thing I need to accomplish with this witness."

Human events are complicated. Complexity multiplies geometrically with each new fact or person in your case. Focus on a limited set of points—your best hand. This takes a lot of thinking and weighing. As in a poker game, if with a particular issue and a particular witness the point you want to make is not really the stronger point, leave it out rather than just trying to ask a question because you feel you should say something about the issue. When you have that one and only one point, map it out. Your preparation map can take the form of a pyramid or iceberg. The tip is the one central important event. Below that event are elements, causes, influences, and persons. For people, map out their motivations, intentions, and where they fit in the struggle to act or resist an act. As you do that, think constantly about the central point at the tip of the iceberg, the one point that rises above all else.

Use simple language and hone your focus

Words are the raw material of cross-examination. In daily practice, always work to use smaller and simpler words, Anglo-Saxon root words rather than longer Latin and Greek terms, words that are sharp, words that are blunt (meaning direct). Every writing, legal writing, and trial advocacy course I have taken (or taught) teaches this. But I see a lot of legal writing, briefs, long pleadings, and letters, and very few of them follow this rule. Why? Maybe it's because complex fact patterns put the brain in the "complicate" mode, or maybe it's because lawyers talk to each other using big words, but for whatever reason, legal writing and speaking naturally slip into long Latinate words and sentences made up of series of clauses that need to be reread or repeated to extract their meaning. Questions in court and in depositions tend to be long rather than short.

In cross-examination, long words, long sentences, and passive-voice sentences are like snakes that will slither between your legs, trip you, and bite you. Translate from lawyer into simple. Always, in everything you write or say, sharpen your words and sentences to express exactly what you mean and nothing more.

If you get up in front of a jury and speak like most lawyers write, you're dead. But if you boil your questions down to the shortest possible length, with the simplest words, several good things happen:

- Your questions will consist of one simple clause that can be easily understood by everyone in the courtroom.

- It will be easier for you to remember your pre-paration, on your feet, without notes.

- Your questions will be more powerful and more memorable.

- It will be easier for both you and the jury to see instantly whether the witness is evading your questions. When the witness gives a long, evasive answer you can say, "I asked you this simple question."

When you ask a simple question you may not get a simple answer, but you can then use that question to press the witness for a simple, truthful answer.

Since your goal is to ask simple, concise questions, it's important that your written documents also be simple and concise. Strunk and White's classical writing guide *The Elements of Style* applies to both legal writing and cross-examination. It promotes a clear and direct style of writing. Whenever I edit legal briefs or prepare my cross-examination or legal arguments I always (1) use short, blunt, direct words, (2) cut out every extra word, and (3) change the passive voice to active.

Simplify enough but not too much

"Make it as simple as possible, but no simpler." This quote, often attributed to Albert Einstein, expresses the essence of the lawyer's task. When in doubt about a line of questioning, lean toward taking it out. More cross-examinations fail by going too far than by not going far enough.

Is there a limit to simplicity? Of course, but you can leave out more than you think, as long as you understand the essence and cover that point. It takes confidence and skill to ask only a few questions. Mental effort spent searching for the line between enough and too much is well spent.

That said, you simplify too much when you leave out relevant facts and open yourself to the charge of omission by your adversary. This is the most common flaw in arguments. Plaintiffs and defendants both leave out facts that contradict their arguments. Focus your cross-examination on the facts that your adversary left out. If you have confronted or neutralized opposing facts that are important, then much of what remains belongs on the cutting-room floor.

Use strategic silence

There is a natural human impulse to fill any social situation with talk, and discomfort with silence. Lawyers especially feel that if they're talking, they're in control of the situation. But many have observed that a well-timed silence is a powerful tool of communication. Just as you must discipline yourself to reduce the overall amount of your documents, your points, and every other aspect of your case, so too must you learn to at times shut off your talking completely and use the power of silence.

Silence is a real and important part of cross-examination. Can you prepare to use strategic silence? You can't predict exactly when you will use it. If it is too rehearsed, it won't be natural and won't work. But if you remain aware of the flow of your cross-examination and avoid the compulsion to fill every moment with speech, you will sense when your silence would have more effect than your words.

Two important situations where strategic silence will help you are positive surprise testimony (when the witness unexpectedly makes a statement that is favorable to your case) and unexpected overreaching by the witness. If there is a positive surprise, a long silence and the proper relaxed posture will emphasize its importance. The witness may realize the mistake and try to correct it, in which case you call that out: "You're trying to take that last statement back?" If the witness has overreached, for example by exaggerating, you pause for a comfortable silence to let it sink in and then you ask questions that push the witness to absurdity.

All cases start out complicated. The art of simplicity is gaining the insight to understand what is important and having the restraint to leave the rest out. Fewer goals, less evidence, fewer exhibits, and fewer, shorter, sharper questions all lead to a powerful simplicity.

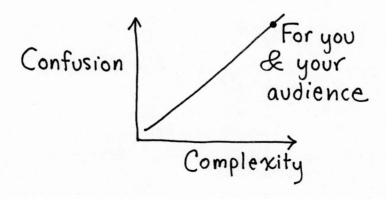

117

Chapter Summary

Main Takeaway

There is more power in simplicity than in complexity. Many cases come down to a single deciding fact, question, or event. Use simple facts and clear statements, documents, and questions to build your case. Seek the shortest path that does the most work.

Earthquake Points

- Simplicity means finding the important thing that connects everything else.

- Constantly ask yourself what you can remove from your case. Discipline yourself to leave out what is not essential.

- Simplicity liberates your intuition, brings you mental clarity and focus, and frees the flow of your cross-examination questions.

- Simplify *everything* in your case: your preparation, documents, goals, pleadings, and cross-examination questions.

- Choose only cross-examination topics that you are likely to win.

- Identify the *one* goal you need to achieve with each witness.

- Use short, blunt, direct English words and short sentences.

- To get a simple, truthful answer from a witness, ask a simple question.

- Learn when to stop talking. Use the power of strategic silence.

CHAPTER 6

STORY

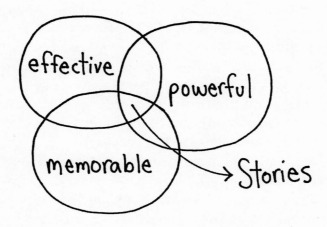

The universe is made of stories, not of atoms.

—Muriel Rukeyser, "The Speed of Darkness"

E VERY CASE TELLS A STORY, and a trial is a contest of
stories. If you find and understand the true story of
your case, then the best strategy and cross-examination
will flow from it. Because the jury will be perceiving
and understanding the trial as a story, not as arguments
and evidence, you should focus on the true story, not on
the better argument. Lawyers who perceive and build
their cases as a story that tells the truth, rather than an
argument to be won, will have the advantage.

There are stories all around us, stories you've read in books and seen in movies and on television. You are involved in some way or another in the story of our nation and current events. There isn't much in your life that doesn't have a story behind it. If language is the main tool of thought, story is the best tool of language. Humans use stories as our primary way of understanding the world around us. Life unfolds in patterns of change and events that connect to form narratives. Life has a beginning and an end. Between those two poles are series of rising and falling waves—the middle story of our life events. Each separate part of your life story has its own beginning, middle, and end. The human mind seeks out these patterns as we try to understand events. They are how we organize the world.

Humans are strongly drawn to stories. They spark powerful emotions and appeal to specific aspects of the human character, like empathy, our sense of justice, competitiveness (winning battles), wanting to do the right thing, wanting to help the underdog, or seeking adventure. Trial stories reflect all of the intense drama and emotion of human life. Much rides on your ability to find the truth at the center of your client's story and reveal it in a compelling way that will connect with the jury's own experience and their common human traits, including their appreciation of moving stories and their need for order. In this chapter I will show you how understanding the elements of story, constructing your case as a story, and presenting it as a story will help you cross-examine intuitively, creatively, and better.

Origins of Cross-Examination in Greek Drama

Greek drama is the basis for the structure of the jury trial. Drama illustrates the interaction of many different story elements: a plot with a conflict and a sequence of parts, actors, dialog, action, emotion, props, the theater, and a chorus representing the community. All of these make an appearance in the jury trial as well.

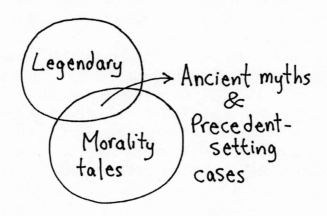

The Greeks invented both drama and the jury trial as a way of resolving important issues in society. Greek drama and the issues it presented were the means of communication about contested issues in the democracy. The protagonist, conflict, antagonist, chorus, crisis, and resolution were all transferred from Greek drama to the form of the jury trial. The word *drama* comes from the Greek word *dran*, meaning to do or to act. Action is at the heart of drama. Greek drama was different from all other literary genres before it in that it combined words and actions. Drama personified conflict: it made the conflicting actors real before the eyes of the community. Two people, the protagonist and the antagonist, stood on a stage having a debate in dialogue. In drama, dialogue moves the plot. Dialogue reveals new information and changes the direction of the story.

The Greeks found drama ideal for working out political conflicts and they adapted it to work out legal conflicts in the form of the adversarial jury trial. In fact, trials were held in the same venue where dramatic plays were produced. The Greek jury trial had a prosecutor, a defendant, and hundreds of jurors. Very often defendants represented themselves. The most famous jury trial we know of from ancient Athens is the trial of Socrates in 399 B.C. on charges of corrupting young people and impious acts. These charges arose from philosophical and political disputes. Socrates, representing himself, cross-examined his prosecutor, Miletus. It was by all accounts a brilliant cross-examination by one of the greatest minds in history. Unfortunately Socrates was convicted and sentenced to death by a jury of his peers—an unhappy and ironic end to the originator of the Socratic method that law schools still use today to teach critical thinking, and an original practitioner, if not the inventor, of what we know as cross-examination.

What Is Story?

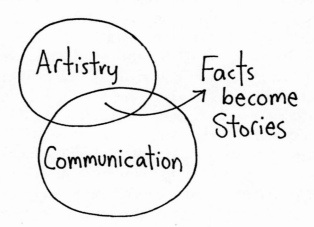

Story is the way that you take disorganized facts and make them useful, comprehensible, true, and persuasive. To do that effectively, you need to understand what makes a good story. It's much more than the facts of the case arranged in order.

Aristotle's work on dramatic theory, *Poetics*, is the first Western work to ask the question, What makes a good story? In it he uses *Oedipus the King* by Sophocles as his prime example of a great story.[1] You may remember from your high school English class that *Oedipus* is the story of a well-meaning man who unwittingly commits the crimes of patricide and incest in fulfillment of a prophecy. If the simple facts of *Oedipus the King* were told chronologically, they would sound like this: Oedipus was abandoned by his parents as a baby because a prophecy told them he would kill his father and marry his mother. But the shepherd they ordered to leave him exposed on a mountain couldn't abandon the infant, and he instead gave Oedipus to a passing messenger. As he grew, Oedipus heard the prophecy about himself, so he left the people he thought were his parents, unknowingly met his real father on the road, got into an argument, and killed him. When he got to the city of Thebes, he solved the riddle of the Sphinx and saved the city from that monster. He was rewarded with marriage to the queen, who turned out to be his mother. When the truth became known, the distraught Oedipus gouged out his eyes and his mother committed suicide.

As a great dramatic story teller, Sophocles does not present these facts in simple chronological order. He masterfully reveals only one small element of the story at a time, *told out of order*, deliberately keeping his audience in suspense until the very end. Very similar to jury trials, the truth in *Oedipus* emerges slowly from a

---

[1] There are unlimited numbers of other great stories. Syd Field, in his book *Screenplay: The Foundations of Screenwriting*, uses the movie *Chinatown* as Aristotle used *Oedipus the King*.

seemingly disconnected series of events that only come together to make sense at the very end of the play.

Oedipus the King is a murder mystery and Oedipus plays a role similar to a prosecutor. He sets about questioning various people to find the murderer. Some evade his questions and others provide bits of the story that, in isolation, don't reveal the murderer's identity. The truth that Oedipus has killed his father and married his mother only comes out when a shepherd who has knowledge of both events is brought to Oedipus to tell his story. Then all of the previously disconnected facts come together and the audience sees the truth.

A narrative is a chronological series of logically connected facts. It is flat in tone and contains no suspense so it doesn't engage the audience emotionally. A great story, in contrast, uses suspense, concealment, and deception, directing attention away from the truth until the opportune moment when the story teller decides to reveal it. In a trial, both you and your adversary, and after opening statements the jury as well, know the framework of the story—how it begins and ends—but in most cases, not how it will get from beginning to end. Cross-examination is the middle part of the story of the trial. In cross-examination witnesses answer each question with facts that piece by piece reveal the whole truth, creating suspense and tension and pulling the judge and jury into the drama, making them want to know the answer to the next question. The witnesses don't know the whole story. Some evade, some divulge important facts that they don't realize are important. Fact by fact, the answers come together to make the story whole.

Great literature and films are crafted around archetypal stories like *Oedipus the King*. They proceed from action to action by the main character. Neither the main character nor the audience knows the big-picture truth of the story. The character forges forward as fact after fact, action after action, hints, and implications pile up until at some point there is a dramatic turn of events accompanied by heightened tension or emotion. The character and the audience see or hear some key piece of information. Suddenly, with the new revelation, all the parts of the story fall into place and make sense.

Similarly, the cross-examiner leads the judge and jury step by step through the story to only one possible conclusion, and suddenly they see the truth clearly. Most trials I have experienced progress in a similar fashion to a turning point. Viewing a story as only the facts of the case doesn't account for everything that happens in the courtroom to pull the story forward to the critical turning point and take the judge and jury to the right conclusion. You and your adversary both enter the courtroom with your sets of facts and evidence that form your stories. But the facts and evidence alone are not sufficient to get you to the outcome you want. What gets you to that outcome is everything that happens from the beginning to the end of the trial. *The trial itself is the story.* The facts, the opening arguments, the witnesses, direct examination, cross-examination, the lawyers, the judge, the objections, the jury and its deliberations: all are part of the story, and the end of the story is unknown until all of these actors have played out their roles. As a "character" in a trial, I also don't know exactly how the trial will end and I can't be sure about the jury's understanding of the big picture. The actors coalesce together to get to the endpoint, and the lawyer needs to manage all of them as part of the story.

You don't control all the facts of the story. Your adversary and the adversary's witnesses are characters who are determined to be part of the story, along with the judge and jury. The members of the jury are not only noting the facts of the case. They are taking in everything that happens in the courtroom—the appearance and demeanor of each player, how the facts are brought out and pieced together, how the adversaries interact with each other. They are reacting emotionally and intellectually as the case unfolds before them, very much like the audience at a Greek drama, and their perceptions become part of the story as well.

In that sense, the most critical part of the story of the case doesn't begin until you enter the courtroom and it doesn't end until the verdict is returned. The story that you constructed during your deep preparation forms the groundwork for the trial, but it is only one piece of the entire trial story. The story of the case unifies all aspects of the trial, both substantive and procedural, form and fact, tone and style.

Story instinct, rather than argument, lets you see the strengths and flaws of the whole of the case, where it is going, and what is missing. Story instinct is the ability to see the facts and events needed for the ending during the story, and to present those so that the jury can, at the right time, see them all come together in a powerful, compelling way.

If you think of story in this broader way as including the facts of the case, your evidence, and your adversary's evidence and story, along with everything that happens in the courtroom, you will have many more parts to work with, and many more possibilities. You can work with the facts, the evidence, your witnesses, the judge and jury, and your adversary. All become elements in the story that you, the storyteller, put forth.

Story Drives the Truth Engine

In chapter 1, I stated that truth is the ultimate goal of our legal system and that it should be at the center of your work as a lawyer. I described cross-examination as a truth engine and defined it as "asking questions that find and reveal the truth." I pointed out that a case turns on some truth at the center.

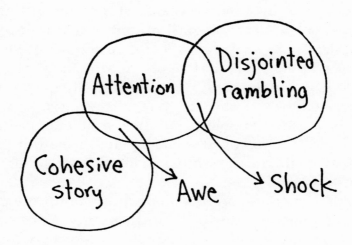

The truth is what is actually happening at any given time from the start of the case to the end. It develops over the course of a case and changes in different contexts, especially during the trial.

A story is the mind's powerful way of learning and comprehending the truth and also, importantly, of persuasion, that is, telling the truth. Story is what will lead you and the judge and jury to that central truth needed for the right verdict. It is what will help you find the truth during your deep preparation, get the witness to reveal the truth during cross-examination, and present it in your closing argument.

Story doesn't only help you *tell* the truth, it helps you *find* the truth. Science and stories are the two most powerful ways that the human brain can find truth. Stories are more effective than science for figuring out human situations outside controlled laboratories. Many court cases involve poor judgment, faulty thinking, irrationality, and emotional motives that stem from common character flaws like greed, jealousy, hubris, and so on. Those are what cause people to end up in conflict. These human failings are better understood by story than by science because stories connect all of the events and psychological processes that lead up to a conflict. So as a lawyer and cross-examiner, if you're rigorous in your fact-finding and in drawing unbiased and logical conclusions, you will be well equipped to understand the true story of your case even if the parties have behaved irrationally and their conflict appears to defy logic. Piecing together the threads of the story will lead you to the relationships among the parts that will make sense of the case.

Cross-examination is a demanding and time-consuming phase of the trial. Judges and juries have high expectations of you. They depend on you to tell a coherent story to help them do their jobs. To do that, you need to choose your topics of cross-examination and witnesses carefully from among the dozens or hundreds of possibilities that make up the case. What topics should you choose, how should you approach them, and in what order should you present them to guide the jury to your essential truth of the case? You find the answers to these questions by understanding the role of story and learning to work with it. By always centering your story around the main principle of truth you will stay focused on what is most important and be able to let go of what is less important.

The very process of using the principles of storytelling to find the true story will make your cross-examination better as you adjust to the free flow of the courtroom and come closer and closer to the truth at the center of your case. Because the story is so powerful— it is what the jury will use to make life-and-death decisions and decisions that make or break people's lives—

you have an ethical responsibility to make it true. Even a story with many true facts could be a false story if there are important parts left out or if the facts are arranged to lead to wrong impressions. Avoid the temptation to put up a false story just because it helps you win. In fact truthful stories are more likely to win, all things being equal.

Stories Are Organic and Fluid

Contrary to what you might be hoping or expecting, the truth and stories are not single, fixed entities. They evolve and change shape through a process of adding new information, putting known facts in new contexts, and developing new insights about them that can continue right up to the last moments of the trial.

Emotion ↑ •Poetry   •Story

•Power Point

→ Logic

The two sides each start out with a number of facts and a theory to account for the facts that is offered by the client or formulated by the lawyer as the narrative that will most easily win the case. It is rare that these initial stories hold up after the discovery of new facts, and if they do, those are the kinds of cases that don't go to trial—they settle or plead.

Anything that involves human beings relating to each other is fluid and difficult to contain and control. Opening and closing arguments are clear and simple, direct and linear. Cross-examination and stories, on the other hand, have ups and downs, twists and turns, unknowns and ambiguities. They might not appear logical on the surface. This inherently organic and fluid nature of stories again makes it clear why story encompasses much more than the facts that you uncover in the beginning.

You, your adversary, the judge, the jury, and the emerging facts all play a role in the courtroom drama, *but you don't have full control over the script*. The opening and closing arguments are set pieces. Direct examination is a rehearsed dialogue with a cooperative actor and each of you can feed lines to the other in advance. But during cross-examination, you don't know exactly what the other actor—the witness you're cross-examining—will say. Moreover, this witness is often trying to undo your story. The witness wants to write a different drama from yours, one that comes to a different climax and resolution from the one you want, turning your happy ending into a tragedy. You can plan your lines in advance, but what if the answers to your questions lead far astray from the script you have drafted? What do you do then?

When the story turns against you, as it will at times, the best reaction is not shock or denial. Try to understand the surprise turn, where it came from and where it's going, and look for facts and ideas that can turn the flow back in your direction. Don't deny it, turn it.

This lack of full control can be unsettling for the lawyer who has prepared the case in a rigid linear way and becomes attached to a single "true" story at the outset. The solution to your insecurity is to accept this fluid characteristic of your case story, flow with it, and make it work to your advantage over your adversary, who is entrenched in an immobile argument and unprepared for new facts. When you understand the story and its structure as a whole, it acts like a map to help you take an alternative route when your planned route is blocked.

The lawyer who sees the advantages in the fluidity of the story and is willing to work to find the truth beneath the surface story has the high ground in the battle of stories. This searching for the truth in the ever-shifting real world of the trial spurs you to become a better lawyer and cross-examiner. This search requires perceiving rather than conceiving, finding and describing concrete vital facts rather than concepts and arguments. You will have the upper hand if you understand that the game of stories is infinite and that you must always be perceiving the changing story yet always skeptical that it represents the final answer.

In other words, you must become fluid yourself and realize that the plans you make at the beginning of your preparation in light of your initial story will need to be modified as the story makes its way gradually toward the truth.

Emotion, Conflict, and Turning Points

Because trial stories are about the human experience and conflict, they contain emotion, even if they seem on the surface to be about something practical and dispassionate. This emotion is shared by everyone in the courtroom and runs the gamut from anxiety to anger, fear, amusement, frustration, boredom, and more. In good stories, emotions come from the artful presentation of the facts and events; but if you force emotion into the jury's face, you become melodramatic and present a bad story. Part of understanding the emotion that a good story evokes is knowing when to leave it out and not force it and to recognize that there is no emotional content in some cases.

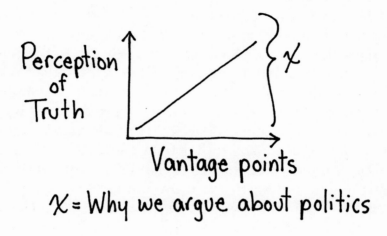

X = Why we argue about politics

Humans love the emotion of stories so much that we make them up for our entertainment, creating elaborate virtual worlds in films and literature. *It is this ability to arouse strong emotions that makes stories so powerful in life and in the courtroom.* The cold facts, while true, don't have the persuasive ability of a well-told story that arouses emotion.

Juries are charged with making impartial decisions about cases by focusing objectively on the facts, but it is undeniable that emotion influences jurors, because to be human is to feel emotion. This is why the back-and-forth of cross-examination is so powerful. It is also why your choice of the facts on which to cross-examine is so important. Sometimes you can bring out undisputed facts that a witness will readily agree to. Then build tension and conflict with the implications and inferences of those facts that a witness may like less and resist more. As the witness resists more, tension rises. Most witnesses resist by evading the question. They give an answer that does not truly answer the whole question and then you must expand a number of questions to get a true answer or to show the jury that the answer was evaded. Getting an answer after the back-and-forth of evasion can be a true deciding point in the trial.

Your choice of answers to pursue and build up to is also important. Witnesses will sometimes evade by giving trivial answers and you waste time, effort, and patience pursuing these answers because the story is harmed and makes no sense. But the buildup to a significant fact, one that illuminates and brings context to the story, is a fine dramatic ending to a cross-examination and can act as a turning point in your case.

Here it's helpful to return to the metaphor of Greek drama. A trial and a dramatic play are both of a slightly lower order of reality than the events they portray. And yet, both provide their audience with a much more complex and sharper experience than simply reading about the events. They bring the audience deeper into the experience, making it as real as possible for them. Their senses are engaged as they see and hear the actors in person. By engaging the senses, a trial heightens the emotions: witnesses, jurors, and spectators at trials often weep. A trial is more than just a story told in words. It helps jurors to not only understand the facts intellectually, but to feel the appropriate emotions that allow them to understand the real impact and meaning of the facts.

Understanding and identifying the true conflict and tension that create emotion is an essential part of your strategy. Jurors will invest attention and emotion in what they believe is real. When you watch a movie, you want the same. You want a sense of reality even though you know it's fiction. Jurors want a story even though they know it's real life. If the story is not real in its action, motivation, and characters, in its events and outcome, you don't like it and aren't willing to accept it as true. Jurors have the same expectation of your case story.

I once participated in a mock jury trial for a case that involved a billion-dollar contract dispute between two media companies. Both companies had billionaire, dominant, imperial-style CEOs whose videotaped depositions were used in the presentation. I played a lawyer on one side, my colleague the adversary lawyer. We each gave our presentations, with, as you would expect, each accusing the other of violating the contract. We then watched three pools of jurors deliberate by closed-circuit television. What each side characterized as a series of wrongs by the other side, these sophisticated Manhattan jurors saw as a fight for market dominance between two egocentric billionaires, using the terms of the contract to support their goals. They were right, and that was the true story at the heart of this case. Ultimately the case went to trial and the winning side told this story and prevailed over the side whose story was based on the victimhood of the wronged party. The truth of most contract disputes is that one side no longer likes the agreement, usually for market or economic reasons, and looks for technical violations to get out of the contract. But lawyers often don't have the insight or the courage to tell this story. The jury in our case could sense the lack of truth in the argument-based case, but was more responsive to the true-story case.

The jury is attracted to the dramatic tension created by conflict among lawyers and witnesses. This dramatic tension pulls the jury into the story so that they have a stake in the outcome and turns the conflict into a living story rather than a didactic parable that leaves the jury unmoved. Strategically you should search for and illuminate these conflicts to keep the tension and the jury's interest high.

Story as Construal of Facts

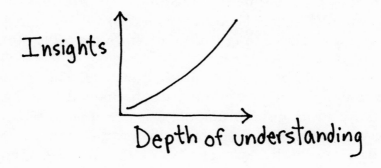

"There are two sides to every story." This truism recognizes that each individual experiences life through perceptions that grow out of the person's unique past experiences, personality, cognitive and emotional style, senses, and so on. The nature of reality is a basic question for physical and social scientists, philosophers, and psychologists. Does objective reality exist apart from people's perceptions? Do you and I see and hear the same things? If we do, why do we report our perceptions differently and why do we make different judgments about what we see and hear?

Juries reach verdicts and judges pass sentences based not only on the facts of the case and the law, but, more importantly, on how they put those facts and laws into stories that they understand as reliable. There may well be dispute about the concrete facts of a case, but it's certain that the parties and the jurors will disagree on the meaning of the facts and the conclusions to be drawn from them. In his book *The Stuff of Thought*[2] Steven Pinker describes the legal dispute surrounding the insurance money due to the owner of the lease on the World Trade Center, Larry Silverstein, after the terrorist attack on September 11, 2001. The buildings were collectively insured for $3.55 billion. Silverstein attempted to collect double the face value of the insurance policies, claiming that the attacks constituted two separate incidents.[3] There was one coordinated attack, but the terrorists brought down two towers. Was this one incident or two?

The case was not actually about facts. There was no reasonable dispute about what happened that day, factually speaking. The dispute was about what Pinker calls the *construal* of those facts, the narrative by which the parties held the facts together and formed them into something understandable—in other words, the story.

Pinker's ideas about the deep connections between thought, human nature, and language apply to many facets of human thinking. It is no accident that they fit what happens in the courtroom like a glove. The strong parallel between his way of conceiving language and the lawyer's work of using language and story to find and reveal the truth to the jury is unmistakable in Pinker's principles of human thought:

- The human mind can construe a particular scenario in multiple ways.

---

[2] Stephen Pinker, *The Stuff of Thought: Language as a Window into Human Nature* (New York: Viking, 2007).

[3] Silverstein eventually won almost $4.6 billion from the insurance companies. He went on to sue American Airlines and United Airlines for $8.5 billion for reckless security at the airports where the hijackers boarded the planes. He lost his nonjury trial in 2013 when the judge ruled that New York State law bars people from being compensated twice for the same loss.

- Each construal is built around a few basic ideas, like "event," "cause," "change," and "intent."

- These ideas can be extended metaphorically to other domains, as when we count events as if they were objects or when we use space as a metaphor for time.

- Each idea has distinctively human quirks that make it useful for reasoning about certain things but that can lead to fallacies and confusions when we try to apply it more broadly.[4]

Pinker's words point to why "objective reality" and "truth" are so elusive and why it's so hard for conflicting parties to agree on a single story. The essence of cross-examination lies in the construal of facts. Both the lawyers and juries construe facts—lawyers according to their trial goals and juries according to their perceptions. In extracting testimony from a witness, the lawyer seeks to create with the jury a shared understanding of truth that uses words to connect and anchor thoughts to events and things in the real world. You must persuade the jury to see your truth as the holistic truth, a unified explanation of everything relevant to the case.

Like the lawyers in the World Trade Center case, you may not be able to dispute many significant facts. Therefore your method on cross-examination will depend on how and where those facts fit into your story structure. Stories rely on a deep understanding of human nature and motivation. How you construe the facts will show the jury the parties' motivations and

---

[4] Pinker, *The Stuff of Thought*, 26.

intent, the causes of events, connections among the facts, the relative importance of each fact in the whole of the story. The story that you build may be based on the same facts as your adversary's story, but how you put them together needs to be different and needs to lead the jury to a different understanding. Which construal of the facts will bind together into the strongest story? Whose mortar will best hold the bricks of the story together, yours or your adversary's?

Story Structure

Although stories are organic and fluid, they nevertheless have a common structure consisting of a beginning, a middle, and an end. As in Greek drama, the structure influences how the story comes out. In the drama of plays, novels, and films the structure of the story can be described as having five parts, sometimes referred to as Freytag's Pyramid after 19th-century German novelist Gustav Freytag: the exposition, rising action, climax or crisis, falling action, and resolution. Those terms give a sense of the rhythm and emotional impact of each part of a story. Each of those parts has specific characteristics. Juries expect you to present a story that follows these common patterns because this is the structure of stories that they understand from their own experiences.

You wouldn't be satisfied to watch a two-hour movie that seemed to go nowhere. You have a strong need for the plot to move in recognizable patterns that carry you along from the beginning, through the middle, to the end. You want to feel your emotions rise to a head at a suspense-filled turning point and then descend at the end when everything becomes clear to you and the conflict is resolved. You want to have a sense of finality at the end of the movie, a feeling that you've under-

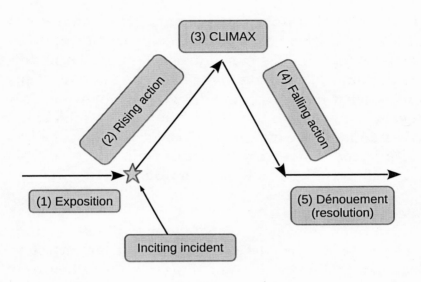

Freitag's Pyramid

stood how things ended up as they did and that the ending makes sense.

Judges and juries have these same needs. As they listen to your case unfolding, they are using their subconscious need for orderly patterns and their need for truth and understanding to make sense of your story. They want you to lay the groundwork for their understanding in the beginning and bring out your supporting facts and evidence in the middle phase of cross-examination. At some point they want to have an "Aha!" moment when you introduce a fact that gives them an important new insight. When you finish your closing argument they want the story to have a clear and logical ending so they can come to the right verdict. Your goal as a lawyer is to provide them with the right experience—the right facts, at the right time, along with the right emotions—to lead them to that point by how you develop your story.

As you plan your cross-examination, make sure you understand where each piece of evidence fits into your story. Avoid mixing things that belong in the middle with things that belong in the beginning or end. Think about what each part of the story is made of: what facts, events, and actions are in the beginning, which are in the middle, and which are in the end. Thinking of a trial as interconnected parts of a story will help you avoid rambling and keep you moving from part to part.

Beats, Scenes, and Acts

Former University of Southern California writing instructor Robert McKee developed a famous story seminar that he has presented to sold-out audiences in the United States and London. Recognizing the importance of stories beyond traditional literature, he adapted his seminar for use by businesses. His ideas are directly related to trial stories and to events in the courtroom. McKee teaches that dramatic structure consists of progressive, cumulative subparts—beats, scenes, and acts. He defines a beat—the smallest element of a story—as "an exchange of behavior in action/reaction. Beat by beat, these changing behaviors shape the turning of a scene."[5] I view cross-examination as the keystone of this story structure. Beats are the "atoms" of stories.

In cross-examination a series of beats builds into a scene, and several scenes come together to form an act. This is a more useful way of visualizing your cross-examination story than as a linear progression of points you want to make one after the other because it groups parts together rhythmically and helps the jury see relationships among facts. When one scene is finished they can

---

[5] Robert McKee, *Story: Substance, Structure, Style and the Principles of Screenwriting* (New York: Harper Collins, 1997), 37.

turn their attention to the next one. Cross-examinations of important witnesses are the scenes that turn the plot of a story and move it forward.

Another advantage of seeing your story this way is that it takes into account the evolution of the story in the courtroom, including the unpredictable behavior of witnesses. A list of points only accounts for your own plans and hopes for how things are going to go; it's harder to adjust it as the action unfolds in the courtroom.

In cross-examination beats are the back-and-forth, question-and-answer exchange between you and the witness, two people moving from positive to negative, or the reverse, like a pendulum. You ask a question to further your story and the witness responds in an attempt to undermine your story. Each time you approach a witness with the goal of making a point, you are working to create a scene of your story. A series of beats rhythmically drums the scene along. Your goal is not necessarily to refute the counterpoint of every answer the witness gives you, but to try to come out ahead even a little bit after each question, confident that each beat is moving you toward a bigger part of the story.

An excellent example of this progression of back-and-forth positive and negative beats is illustrated by a scene in the film *Silence of the Lambs* between Jodie Foster as young FBI Agent Clarice Starling and Anthony Hopkins as the psycho-genius serial murderer Hannibal Lecter. In this scene Starling introduces herself to Lecter in his prison cell and asks to speak with him. He asks to see her credentials and then seductively lures her closer to examine them. "This expires in one week," he says. "You're not real FBI, are you?" Initially it appears that Lecter has the upper hand, as he makes her sit down so he is looking down on her and takes control of the conversation. But throughout the scene the balance of power shifts subtly back and forth between them as they try to control each other psychologically with carefully chosen words, gestures, and facial expressions. Ultimately Lecter prevails when he suddenly ends the conversation by closing the glass door of his cell, shutting Starling out and dismissing her with "You fly back to school now, little Starling." Throughout the film Starling and Lecter jockey for control in these tit-for-tat exchanges as the film comes closer and closer to the revelation of the identity and location of the serial killer Buffalo Bill.

Film critic Tony Zhou analyzes the above scene in an excellent short video entitled *"Silence of the Lambs*: Who Wins the Scene?"[6] His comment on the shifting balance of power as the pendulum beats back and forth exactly expresses the interaction between cross-examiner and witness: "In drama, two characters walk into a room. Each wants something from the other. The question of the scene is: who gets what they want?" In this instance Zhou gives the win to Lecter, but in other scenes Starling scores some victories.

Lecter and Starling's verbal maneuvering is very similar to a good cross-examination. You want to write and act in a scene that you win. You walk into a room with information, prepared topics, and the opportunity to ask questions. You want something. The witness also has information, and possibly a plan or strategy to prevent you from getting what you want. The scene begins with your first question. Whether you win or not depends on your ability to perceive the witness's strategy and move closer to your goal with each question. Similar to the advantage of the first move in chess, notice that it is Lecter who asks the first significant

---

[6] https://www.youtube.com/watch?v=5V-k-p4wzxg

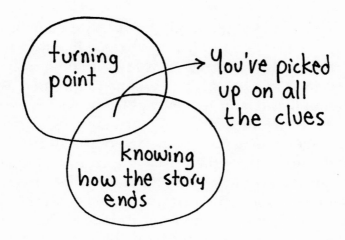

question, "May I see your credentials?" He then gains power with perceptive observations, small facts that reveal some truth about Agent Starling that she might prefer to not reveal. But Starling does walk away with the information she seeks, so the scene is not a total loss for her. This illustrates that you don't need to win each beat of a scene, nor even the scene as a whole, in order to get some benefit from it if your small wins are moving your story forward.

Crisis: The Turning Point

Every trial story, like a Greek drama, has a turning point, a crisis. The crisis is of particular interest to the cross-examiner. The Greek word *krisis* originally meant "decision" or "judgment." In Middle English it came to mean a decisive point, specifically the turning point in a disease, where the patient would either start to get better or die. This point is where cross-examination is most valuable, and where you should search for opportunities to turn the course of the trial.

Your adversary's direct examination establishes one side of the story in the jurors' minds. Cross-examination reveals new information that becomes a turning point, changing the plot and the jury's previous under-standing of things and moving the trial in a new direc-tion. It often comes down to a few or sometimes just one essential fact that you may hone to question a wit-ness about for an hour to finally get it out. A key witness has left out or mistaken a fact, or new facts come out that change the perception, the arc, of the story.

You can think of the crisis as a crossroad, a point where the trial could go in several different directions, as when a character in a film is forced to decide how to react to a crisis by choosing from possible courses of action. It's a suspenseful moment as the jury waits to see what direction you will take and how the wit-ness will respond to your efforts. It's important that you take charge here and not lose this opportunity to gain a stronger foothold. When you arrive at this cross-road it may be new terrain for you because as I have emphasized, the plans you made during preparation are now changed by the unpredictability of the other side's strategies and the witness's behavior. If you stay close to your view of the whole story, you will be able to choose your questions at this critical turning point by fit-ting them into the structure of other facts and testimony that have come out.

The information that makes this critical turning point is often present from the beginning of the story, although you may not detect it initially or understand its importance. When you see that revelation in a great story in literature or film, you look back and realize that it was laid out from the start. A great example of this is Harper Lee's 1960 novel *To Kill a Mockingbird*, about the involvement of lawyer Atticus Finch and his two children in a racially motivated false accusation of rape against a black man. The character called Boo Radley is mysterious and frightening to the Finch children. Yet there are a few subtle clues, like small presents left in trees for the children, that could cause the reader to question that surface perception if the reader is paying attention. In the end Boo Radley risks his life to save the Finch children. The revelation that Boo is not dangerous but only painfully shy is a compelling part of that great story. The information to understand the ending of the story is present from the beginning for the reader who is able to recognize it.

It requires a deep understanding of both your case and human nature to identify and articulate the facts and questions that will turn your case. They are usually not apparent on the surface, but if you take the time to make connections and look beyond the obvious you will gain this insight.

How to Make the Story and Make It Work for You

You begin developing a story of the case the first time you talk to a client. Your client will usually offer a theory of the case: "mistaken identity" or "If they had told me the truth, I never would have invested in that scheme." This is the first opportunity for you to separate facts and possible facts from opinions, and group or connect facts as causes of other facts. Take your client's theory at your own risk. The first story that suggests itself is usually not the true story, and it will take quite a bit of digging and thinking to find the true story and decide how to present it for strongest impact.

Stories, especially true stories, are discovered and perceived before they are told. Once you have discovered the "atoms," the facts of the case, then you examine and think about these facts until the true story of the case emerges to you out of the way they come together to form logical and truthful inferences, conclusions, and narratives.

145

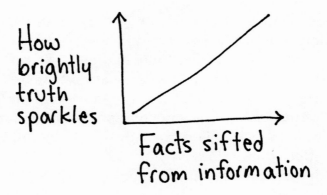

How
brightly
truth
sparkles

Facts sifted
from information

Create a story using Big Facts and make it compelling

The hard part is not finding the story, but finding the most complete and compelling true story, which is hardly ever the first story that the facts suggest. If you have broken your case down into its atomic parts, then the right story has probably suggested itself to you. Big Facts—from documents, photos, witnesses, and physical evidence, including the scene of the incident—are strong signposts directing you to the story of the case.

Sometimes the unfavorable Big Facts, alone or in combination, are simply too big to confront or work around. Those are cases where settlement or plea should be your strategy, not cross-examination. But when the facts create and compel favorable connections and themes in your story, you can begin to imagine their presentation at trial.

Big Facts are those that can't be disputed and that compel a jury to draw certain conclusions. If you ignore these facts and try to tell a story without them, the story will not be true. Big Facts are the case's driving force. There are always small facts that flow against the vein, but they cannot defeat the juggernaut of the Big Facts. Therefore you must craft your story to take in *all* of the Big Facts or go around them by showing that they are not needed for the jury to make a decision.

It is a loser's game to try to deny a fact that you cannot reasonably deny. You will just lose your credibility. But an important aspect of storytelling is that the surface of the story does not show what is deep within it. In well-told stories, first appearances and the obvious give way to deeper unseen truths. So though you cannot dispute facts that on their surface seem bad for your case, the inferences and conclusions that they lead to may be different from what is obvious.

As you weave your story, a useful mental exercise is to list the facts that are favorable to each side. Identify which of your favorable facts your opponent disputes. Draw inferences from the facts that are undisputed by either side that can win your case. Sometimes with story-based thinking you can draw inferences or context favorable to you from facts that on first look seemed bad.

Compelling stories are fact driven as well as visual, tactile, and vivid, drawing in your listeners and causing them to suspend disbelief in the same manner as good fiction. A good story is clear and sharp rather than vague and conclusory. You achieve that by making it out of indisputable facts, and by understanding the overall themes and details of your adversary's story so that your story stands out clearly against the other side's. A story that relies on conclusions and arguments is weak and will not be vivid to the listener. A story that supports conclusions and generalities with facts and evidence is a well-made story. You must find the truest, most persuasive story that encompasses everything that is important and leaves no subplots unresolved.

Tell a story by showing short, simple facts

Remember that Big Facts are made up of a series of short, simple facts. The best way to bring your story to life in cross-examination is to use the tried-and-true classic method of asking the witness a series of simple factual questions that appear on their surface to be unrelated to each other or to an overarching story.

Guide the judge and jury through your story arc

A story arc is the progression of the parts of the story described above: beginning (exposition), rising action, climax or crisis, falling action, and resolution. In the complex and changing back-and-forth of cross-examination questions, new evidence, and series of witnesses, the jury can lose sight of your story arc. They depend on you to lead them logically through your story. You need to make sure that your story follows its arc even as you adjust it for new events in the courtroom, and that the jury knows where you are in the story arc. The challenge is to keep this arc visible to the jury without allowing your witnesses to know and manipulate the direction or outcome of the scene that you share with them.

With the topics and facts that you choose to ask about, you are the writer who guides the story toward your summation. Unlike characters in a movie, you have an awareness of the story and its goals. You may not be able to predict exactly what each witness will say or how the jury will perceive the evidence and decide the case, but you know your plot and where you want it to end up. As the storyteller you have a higher level of knowledge than any individual witness or the jury and you are pulling—sometimes gently, sometimes more forcefully—the other characters in the scene along your plotline.

You always want the jury to have a hint of where you're going. Your early statements should anticipate and foreshadow your summation and the judge's instructions, which are the last words the jury will hear before they deliberate. This foreshadowing gives them an anchor so that they understand the progression of your story.

Show, don't tell: give facts, not theories or explanations

In his book *Story* Robert McKee writes that storytelling is "the creative demonstration of truth. A story is living proof of an idea, the conversion of idea to action. A story's event structure is the means by which you express, then prove your idea without explanation."[7] The phrase "prove your idea without explanation" is the key to understanding stories for lawyers. It is sometimes expressed as "Show, don't tell." The best cross-examinations, the best trial strategies, the best summations show the truth of what happened by accumulated facts arranged in a particular way. Flawed cross-examinations attempt to tell a narrative during the questioning, or to argue a point by explaining instead of simply proving facts. Showing is more effective than telling because it draws the jury powerfully into your story and it gives jurors the evidence they need directly from the witness rather than secondhand from you.

Know the end of your story and pull it toward the end

The common way of working with the story is to "push" it from behind with laboriously prepared lists of points, outlines, and questions. When you're bound to such preset plans you're less able to react fluidly to the story as it evolves in the courtroom, and more likely to be caught off guard by unexpected events that weren't in your plan. It's hard to keep your eye on your ultimate goal when you're separated from that goal by an

---

[7] McKee, *Story*, 113.

elaborate preconceived list of questions you need to get through. As witnesses fail to give you the answers you were hoping for, you find yourself going off track and scrambling to get back to your list of written questions. This occupies most of your mental effort and meanwhile you've lost sight of your end goal. No great cross-examiner prepares a list of questions and then blindly adheres to it.

A better approach is to imagine yourself standing at the end of the story, at the point where you have given the jury everything they need for the right verdict. Look backward and pull the strands of the story toward the end that you know has happened. There are several advantages to this approach. The first is that you can see the whole trial at once, like a quarterback or a general surveying the whole field. A general moves to high ground to view the terrain and the opposing forces. He sees the battle coming to him, the points where the forces contest, the back-and-forth movement of each side, and where the line may break.

If you have a strong image of where you want the trial to end, your intuition will engage and you will react to events as they happen and be able to shape the story to your desired end. If your story gets off track, you can see and correct this to make sure that the trial will finish where it's supposed to, right where you're standing at the endpoint. You will waste less effort and keep the story on its most efficient arc to its conclusion. To use this method you must know where you're going from the start. One of the best trial techniques I ever learned is to write out your closing argument before you start the trial. This is a well-known practice and doing it is a bedrock for good cross-examination. Writing your summation disciplines you to focus on the big picture and the big facts that compel the ending of your story, which you usually know at the beginning.

It forces you to argue favorable big facts and to address or refute unfavorable big facts. Normally cross-examination focuses on the connections that weave the big facts into a narrative. Knowing your summation gives your presentation of evidence, especially cross-examination, definition and focus. At the end of the case the jury will have many questions as they go into deliberation. The closing argument presents questions for the jury, the answers to which have already been provided by the evidence in the case. The job of summation is to show the jury how the evidence provides the answers.

Knowing the points that you intend to accomplish in cross-examination gives you firmness of strategy, but flexibility of tactics. If there is surprise testimony, you will be able to weave it into your important points, and be much better prepared to deal with surprise.

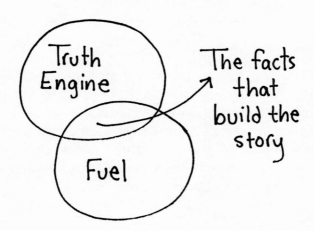

But be careful: good storytellers don't tell the ending at the start of the story. They are artful and strategic in how they reveal each new fact and how they arrange both good facts and bad facts within the story. They deploy their story strategically.

Thinking and planning your case as a story, a drama, will give you an intuitive advantage over the lawyer who thinks in terms of theories and arguments. The process of drawing the truest, most complete story out of the facts will create the most persuasive case and allow your mind to search for and find the best cross-examination questions in any back-and-forth scene. It is just more natural to think, speak, and reply to another human being in story mode than in argument mode. Story thinking will also get deeper into the human-nature aspects of events and reveal connections and truths that the argument method will not.

If you use the principles of strategy to make your story and your scenes and lines, you will be able to maneuver your story to its happy ending.

CHAPTER SUMMARY

Main Takeaway

A trial is a contest of stories and you are a story teller. Stories are more compelling to the jury than arguments and evidence because they arouse emotions connected to human experience and help the jury make sense of events. Use your cross-examination to find and reveal the story at the heart of your case.

Earthquake Points

- The trial is a story with a beginning, middle, and end and rising and falling drama. The end of the trial story is unknown until the judge gives a verdict.

- Center your story of the case around the main principle of truth. There is more than one true story path.

- The story of the case is not fixed. It evolves organically throughout your preparation and all phases of the trial.

- Learn to be comfortable with the fact that you don't have full control over the script of the story because you can't control what your adversary, witnesses, and the judge are going to do. Be prepared to change your plans and work flexibly with the story as it develops in the courtroom.

- In cross-examination you construct the story of the case by asking questions, each of which reveals one piece of the story.

- Most trials have a turning point in the story where a witness reveals a key piece of information that uncovers the truth. Focus your cross-examination on getting to this turning point.

- Write your closing argument before the trial, imagine yourself at the end of your story, and then during cross-examination pull the threads of the story toward that desired end. When a witness pushes your story off course, bring it back to your end goal.

- Don't reveal the end of the story to the witness. Get the witness to disclose the facts without knowing how they're being using to build your story.

CHAPTER 7

STRATEGY

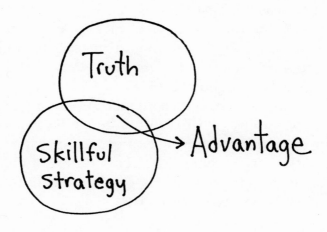

Tell all the truth but tell it slant—
Success in Circuit lies
Too bright for our infirm Delight
The Truth's superb surprise
As Lightning to the Children eased
With explanation kind
The Truth must dazzle gradually
Or every man be blind—

—Emily Dickinson

A TRIAL IS A BATTLE OF STORIES: your story versus your opponent's. To come out on top in this battle, you need to effectively use strategies for winning contests. As with story, truth clumsily presented against a strategically presented deception is at a disadvantage.

In fact, without strategy, you may not even be able to present parts of the truth. The framework of stories and the principles of strategy are the best tools for making decisions about who, when, and on what subjects to cross-examine. Strategy shows you how to bring out a specific fact so that the jury can place it into their own story of the case to best effect.

Many principles of legal strategy are used in a variety of other contests, including sports, military campaigns, politics, marketing, and games like chess and cards. Studying these ideas outside the realm of law and trials will give you a deeper understanding and help you come up with creative and effective strategies for presenting your case, cross-examination, and the trial itself. This chapter presents the essential principles of cross-examination strategy in terms of winning a contest between two adversaries.

"All Warfare Is Deception"

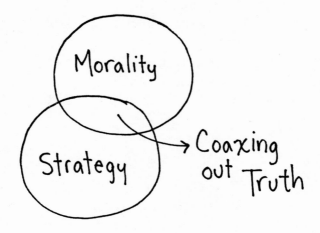

Chinese general Sun Tzu begins his famous work on strategy, *The Art of War*, with the statement, "All warfare is deception." Indeed, strategy must be based on some kind of deception. But I've been talking about cross-examination as a way of revealing truth, and claiming that pursuing truth is the best strategy. How can these two ideas of truth and deception be reconciled?

If people readily told the truth we would have far fewer lawsuits or they would be settled out of court. The reality is that witnesses who are lying, biased, or mistaken but sticking to their mistakes will not give up the truth voluntarily. When I refer to strategy as deception, I don't mean lying or misleading. I mean doing what you need to do to bring out the truth, for example by not letting the witness know exactly where the story is coming from or going, or letting a witness believe you're seeking or emphasizing certain facts or conclusions when you're really pursuing some other goal. I believe that this kind of misdirection of the witness's attention—not lying or misrepresenting—is ethical when pursuing the truth, since the goal is to lead a reluctant witness to tell the truth. It is simply a means of countering the witness's own deception. Just because you're seeking the truth doesn't mean you have to put yourself at a disadvantage in the contest by failing to use all truth-seeking strategies at your disposal.

A good strategist wins a contest regardless of whether the victory is moral or not. There is no moral outcome of a chess match or a poker game as long as skill and stealth rather than cheating have been used. Evil leaders can win wars if they are superior strategists. Other than excellence at the game itself, the object of the game strategist is to win, not to search for truth or impart values to society. But there is a moral component in law and trials, and as we have discussed, this value element gives an advantage to the story-teller and strategist who is also a truth-seeker. Lawyers use stealth and deception in service to the truth that is the goal of our justice system. Some form of deception is necessary to counterbalance the natural human tendency of witnesses to distort the truth in service to their own goals. In this chapter strategic deception is presented in this positive sense.

Strength versus Stealth

There are two basic approaches to winning all kinds of contests: strength and stealth. Strategy is a plan to win by stealth rather than strength. This means planning and executing your cross-examination goals not by frontal attack, but by indirection, deception, and an unexpected approach.

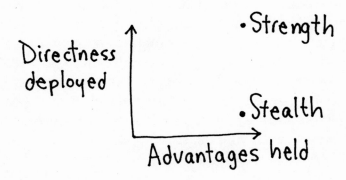

Confrontational cross-examination is a direct frontal attack. You believe a witness is lying and you overtly state that the witness is lying. If you have a sworn statement directly contradicting the witness's present testimony, or a video or audio tape showing clearly that the witness is lying, your strategy is simple: you can win by a frontal attack, on the strength of your evidence, and by the proper application of outright contradiction.

A frontal attack has its place in cross-examination, but only under specific circumstances: you must have superior strength or positioning. You must be certain that you "have the goods" on your adversary. A direct attack carries risk if you fail, so you must make sure your evidence truly contradicts the witness and take great care that the witness does not wiggle out of the contradiction.

In some trials, the evidence overwhelmingly favors one side and that side will generally win regardless of the adversary's strategic skill. But often in life, war, and trials, overwhelming strength is not the rule, in part because when there is a clear winner the losing party tends to avoid battle and seek some other course, such as "suing for peace," capitulating, or withdrawing. Cases that are very clearly in one party's favor tend to be settled out of court, so that in cases that do go to trial, often contestants are more evenly matched in strength. In these cases the slightly weaker side can win by using superior strategy, meaning stealth.

Strength is a simpler, less calculated approach requiring less strategic skill. In criminal cases, prosecutors often have the luxury of using strength as their main strategy while defense attorneys may need to use stealth. A prosecutor can rely on evidence in place of deceptive strategy: witnesses, photos, and in most cases some physical evidence. Prosecutors as well as civil plaintiffs' attorneys can pick and choose their cases, winnowing out those with significant weaknesses that would make them difficult to win. Thus their cases have strength at the outset. Their strategy is to be direct and organized and to tell the story using its simplest and most unassailable and defensible line. In criminal cases the defense is really the "attacker," attempting to defeat the prosecutor's story. Thus prosecutors seek to avoid allowing defendants to use strategy against them.

The defense has a much greater need for strategy. The majority of criminal defense cases are made up of cross-examination alone. In most cases prosecution witnesses will not willingly help the defense, so the defense must advance its case strategically by not revealing its goal or storyline outright to the witnesses.

Using strategy, you can win points where you lack strong evidence. Strategy allows those with less apparent strength to overcome those with more. Regardless of which strategy you choose, make sure that the strength of your attack is proportional to the importance of the fact or witness to the story. Weak attacks on an important witness are just as harmful as disproportionately dramatic or angry attacks on a peripheral witness or fact.

The Indirect Approach

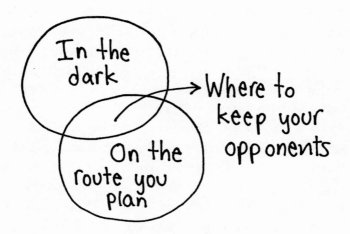

Lawyers can learn a great deal from military strategists. Basil Henry Liddell Hart (1895–1970) was a British infantry officer who fought in the World War I Battle of the Somme, which saw more than a million casualties, including 60,000 British troops who were killed on the first day of the campaign. Based on his experiences in World War I and his study of military history — including military leaders such as Sun Tzu, Napoleon, and General Sherman — Liddell Hart developed a set of principles for winning military conflicts (reviewed at the end of this chapter). He was strongly opposed to frontal assault as a military strategy, attributing Britain's loss of more than 600,000 soldiers in the Great War to this approach. He rather advocated using indirect strategies to achieve military goals, writing, "In strategy the longest way round is often the shortest way there; a direct approach to the object exhausts the attacker and hardens the resistance by compression, whereas an indirect approach loosens the defender's hold by upsetting his balance."[1] To upset the enemy's balance Liddell Hart recommended concealing one's intentions, initially dispersing forces to later concentrate them at the right time, and using the element of surprise.

In cross-examination, the essence of strategy is this indirect path described by Liddell Hart. It is the path of least resistance, approaching your objective from the side, not head on. Deception in strategy is indirection, not letting your adversary know exactly how you will get to your goal.

The indirect approach means figuring out how to get to your goal while avoiding your adversary's strong points, or skillfully orienting your strong points against the adversary's weak points. It means masking your plans and intentions so that your opponent can't mobilize strengths to counter you. It means finding the path of least resistance and least expectation, so that

---

[1] *Strategy*, 2nd rev. ed. (New York: Meridian, 1991), 5.

when you reveal your goal—your holistic story of truth that encompasses all of the facts—it has been hidden in plain sight. The principles and examples of indirect strategy are presented below.

Fragment your story to disperse your forces

The indirect approach in cross-examination is an essential aspect of the art of storytelling. In literature and film, writers don't have to contend with an opponent trying to undo their story as they tell it. But storytelling in cross-examination happens within an adversarial contest in which the main goal is to defeat the other party's story. Following the military strategy of dispersing forces to distract the enemy, a main goal of cross-examination is to fragment your own story—that is, to bring out the discrete facts without allowing witnesses to make their own story out of them. If you reveal your story, the witness will try to counter it. You must have the discipline to keep these facts fragmented or disjointed so that you're not revealing the plot or narrative of your story. For example, when you need two points to make a compelling argument, you could pursue one point each with two different witnesses, even suggesting that your position on the other point, the one you are not asking the witness about, is the opposite of what it really is.

Your facts are like a general's forces. When you ask a series of questions about apparently unrelated facts, you're dispersing your forces to deceive the enemy about your intentions. In warfare, a concentration of forces in one place tells the adversary where your strength is and what your intentions are. In cross-examination, putting a number of facts together into a coherent point does the same thing. Good generals disperse their forces until just before the attack. This deception leads adversaries to forgo resistance on what they consider to be minor or negligible gains for you. By choosing and ordering the facts in such a way as to make them appear unrelated to your ultimate objective, you make them nonthreatening. Witnesses let their guard down and answer more spontaneously, rather than carefully calculating how their answers will impact their position.

Lawyers who use the classic method of cross-examination—figuring out what essential facts are needed to tell the story in their closing argument and asking those facts on cross-examination—are employing what Liddell Hart highlighted as the single most important element of strategic warfare: concentration. He explains how to achieve concentration by counterintuitive means. First you spread your forces along a line that the enemy would expect. This draws the enemy's attention to those points and forces him to deploy his troops along that line. Then when you are ready to attack, you concentrate your force in the area least likely to be defended by the enemy. The classic method of cross-examination and Liddell Hart's definition of strategy are the same!

Don't let witnesses know the part they're playing

It is your witnesses who construct your story, one scene at a time. But unlike characters in a movie, who know ahead of time exactly how the movie will end and what role they will play in bringing the story to that end, with the indirect approach your witnesses must not see your plot, how you intend to end your story, and the role they will play in helping you do it. Otherwise they will foil your plans.

To help you construct your story, your witnesses simply need to give up specific facts and agree with each small element of your plot. It's not necessary for the jury to see a coherent story emerging from the testimony of each witness—that will happen in your summation. In cross-examination it's only important that the jury hear the witness confirm each small bit of the story. In the previous chapter we saw that a story is made up of beats, scenes, and acts. No single witness will provide all the information to construct a scene or an act smoothly. The witness's role is to reveal the single beats that are needed for your final story.

The success of this indirect approach depends on keeping witnesses unaware of how their answers will ultimately be used, which depends on your skillful direction of the witness's attention away from your real intent. Like the military strategist, you spread out your facts so as to not draw attention to their importance in the whole story and you get the unsuspecting witness to confirm them. You intentionally disjoint the pieces of the story so that your questions don't seem to be leading to any particular point. The witness just thinks you're asking for one unrelated fact after another, each bearing no apparent relation to the previous one. The witness doesn't perceive the importance of these facts in isolation.

The witness's resistance is now lowered. Your cross-examination proceeds unemotionally. This is the safest way of collecting the facts you need because it protects you from the damaging answers that witnesses give when they are aware of your adversarial intent and realize that they can derail it. If they feel the mounting tension of a story that is appearing increasingly unfavorable to them, they will naturally resist your efforts.

Each fact is like a stone that you lay in a stream in order to cross to the other side. In cross-examination you lay the stones randomly so that witnesses don't understand how they're helping you make your case and they willingly give you each small stone. If your narrative is creative and obscure enough, even an otherwise hostile witness will help you.

Of course the witness will sometimes figure out where you're going. When that happens, focus your questions on your strongest facts, ones that the witness can't deny without losing credibility. The best technique is to ask only about simple facts, preferably not in any order that allows the witness to figure out what your real story is.

Regroup your forces in your summation

In your summation you have the advantage of maximum control over your story. Now there are no witnesses to counter your story, resist telling the truth, evade your questions, or spin the facts. Your witnesses have played their part by unwittingly providing you with the facts you need. Like a military strategist, you now concentrate your forces into a coherent and powerful story in front of the jury. You rearrange the facts into a narrative that wins your case.

I have often watched great cross-examiners at work as they gather the small facts of their case, and I often say to myself, "That doesn't look like anything special." It's not loud, dramatic, or intense. But when it all comes together on summation, it is a masterpiece of control of the complete drama.

Prove facts on cross- rather than direct examination

Direct examination is exactly what the term indicates: a means of asking a witness direct questions to bring out the main facts of the case. In cross-examination a less direct approach is often required in order to get the jury to make the right inferences by making disputed facts fit with the undisputed big facts.

Juries consider a fact admitted by a witness on cross-examination reliable since they don't have to take just one side's word that the fact is true—both sides state that it is true. Facts you prove on cross-examination are better than facts proven on direct. A battle is not won until the fact that serves your story is revealed in cross-examination. The most successful cross-examinations are those in which you can get either hostile or neutral witnesses to agree willingly to a number of facts, each one of which does not win the case, but when put together in your summation make a winning case.

The key to this technique is that the witness doesn't know where you're going with your story, and yet you move the plot forward. This is a very effective approach because it confines the witness's role to your own goals and gets facts from witnesses that they don't realize are harmful to their case. Moreover, it's an interesting and dramatic technique.

Proving facts on cross-examination is consistent with a truism of all juries: the fewer conflicts jurors have to resolve, the happier they are. Juries like lawyers who catch liars, but what they like most is a lawyer who makes their job easy. They want a narrative that fits the facts that both sides agree on. They want to reach their verdict without making tough credibility decisions. Using the indirect approach to get witnesses to admit facts in cross-examination is the best way to establish a mutually agreed upon set of facts for the jury. You will then incorporate these acknowledged facts into your story rather than attacking them or having to explain them away.

Examples of the Indirect Approach in Criminal Trials

In our first example of a criminal case, your client, the defendant, is found standing over the dead victim when the police arrive on the scene. The coroner's report shows five bullet wounds in the victim and the angle of entry of the bullets. Your client pleads self-defense. The jury is not inclined to doubt the credibility of the arresting officers who found him standing over the dead man, or the coroner's report. You must somehow incorporate the big fact of your defendant's presence near the corpse and the bullet holes without forcing the jury to decide which side is lying. You can't dispute the five bullet holes. You need to work with the facts that neither side can dispute. In this case you can use the coroner's report and his cross-examination testimony to show that the wound entry angles are consistent with the defendant's statement that the victim jumped him and was on top of him when he was fighting for his life. Then the coroner's report becomes a positive big fact that supports your story. This approach allows the jury to accept the facts presented by both the police and the coroner. They prefer to reach a verdict along this path, rather than along a path that requires them to decide disputed facts and disputed witness credibility.

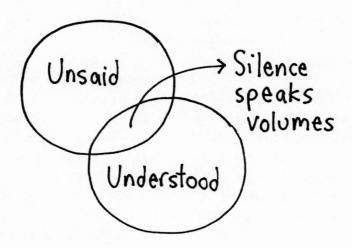

Our second example shows how to conceal your intent by having two goals for a question: a positive direct goal and a negative or indirect goal. In the simplest form the positive goal is to gain an admission if the witness agrees to the fact in your question. If the witness evades your question or denies a true fact, your negative or indirect goal is to show that the witness isn't credible.

I once had a client who was a defendant in a murder case. He had made a statement admitting to possessing a revolver similar to the murder weapon. In his statement he said that he lent a .25 revolver to a friend, and when the friend returned the pistol there was one spent shell in the chamber, which can be seen in a revolver by flipping out the cylindrical chamber that holds the bullets. But the deceased had been shot twice.

During the cross-examination of a hostile and highly experienced detective, I got him to explain to the jury that all the shells stay in the chamber after the revolver is fired until you empty them out yourself. He did not know where I was going with this, but his ego made him very willing to show off his knowledge of firearms and explain the operation of revolvers to the jury. I took an indirect approach to the witness by asking questions that appealed to his positive qualities of competence and knowledge in order to get to the real goal of showing that he had manipulated my client's confession. The detective was not aware of the significance of the information he was revealing. He willingly explained that if the gun has a revolving chamber, and there is only one spent shell, that clearly means that only one shot was fired. I never questioned the detective about how many shots had killed the deceased.

When the medical examiner testified, I asked how many shots killed the deceased. She answered, "Two." I could hear the jurors gasp in realization that there was a major inconsistency between my client's statement—the centerpiece of the prosecution's case—and the physical evidence of the medical examiner. My client was acquitted of murder.

Example of the Indirect Approach in a Civil Case

The following example from a civil case[2] offers a difficult problem involving the passage of time and the witness's memory. This case shows how the lawyer's careful indirect strategic approach can make the difference between obscuring and revealing the truth by avoiding the temptation of the simpler, more direct path that could end in an impasse.

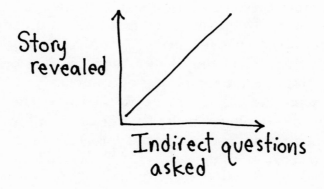

In this case, a company in financial distress took out a loan for $350 million. One term of the loan that the case turned on allowed the bank to go after the company's subsidiaries if the company defaulted on the loan. The CEO, desperate to get money from the bank, agreed to the onerous loan terms. The existence of the guarantee triggered a massive tax liability, which demolished the finances of the company and pushed it into bankruptcy. The company's shareholders brought suit against the CEO for making false statements about the company's finances.

---

[2] This was a real case, in which I represented the witness. To illustrate my principles I have created the questions that I would have asked had I been the questioner and representing the other side.

169

The question at trial was whether the CEO of the company knew that this important term had been added to the loan agreement, making the loan more burdensome on the company and more favorable to the bank. The CEO denied that he was aware of this term. An added complication to the questioning is that the deposition took place about ten years after the event.

The witness here is the treasurer of the company who had negotiated the loan. The witness appeared to be honest but legitimately could not remember conversations from ten years ago—not uncommon in many civil cases where deposition takes place a number of years after the events in question. The goal here is to somehow reconstruct the likely events in spite of the witness's imperfect memory and his reluctance to comment on what the CEO knew or didn't know. The first part of the questioning, which I have created for the purpose of illustration, uses a direct approach to establish as many facts as possible.

Q: You negotiated the loan document, correct?

A: Yes.

Q You knew that the subsidiary guarantee term was not supposed to be in the loan agreement, right?

A: Yes.

Q: The CEO knew that?

A: I assume he did.

Q: Did he ever tell you that?

A: I don't remember.

Q: I'm showing you the loan document draft. Do you see that on page 23 the words "subsidiary guarantee" are crossed out?

A: Yes.

Q: The initials next to the cross-out are yours?

A: Yes.

Q: I'm showing you a second document, labeled "Issue List." You made this list?

A: Yes.

Q: The first term on the issue list is "subsidiary guarantee."

A: Yes.

Q: You discussed the issue list with the CEO?

A: I don't remember.

Q: It was your practice to meet with the CEO and tell him about the negotiations?

A: It was my practice to meet with him the next day and tell him about the negotiations.

Q: The issue list was prepared for that meeting?

A: Yes.

Q: So you discussed the subsidiary guarantee provision, that the banks wanted to insert, with the CEO?

A: I don't remember.

Imagining that you're the cross-examiner in this case, you're now at a point where a generally honest and cooperative witness has given you something, but maybe not enough to prove even civilly that the CEO knew about the bad loan term. There is no point in further direct questions like "Are you telling me the CEO really didn't know about this bad loan term?" You will only get the same noncommittal answers and antagonize the witness.

One way around this impasse would be to ask the treasurer a number of questions about whether the CEO was competent, did his job diligently, read papers before signing them, and so on, in an attempt to show that he knew what he was doing. This is the "knave or fool" technique: showing that a person is either deceitful or incompetent. But you might hit a dead end with this approach if the treasurer says, "I don't know. He was my boss, I wasn't his. I didn't follow him around and supervise him."

The indirect strategy to overcome the treasurer's lack of memory in a nonobvious way is to focus on the treasurer himself and not the CEO. You ask the treasurer about his knowledge and competence and focus on the $350 million loan document and its importance to the company. You ask him about his diligence in noting and writing down the new terms and the problematic terms in the document and his diligence in doing his job to make sure the CEO was properly informed. That is your indirect goal. The witness will most likely give you the answers you need as he is anxious to confirm his competence and right actions.

Once you've gotten answers from the treasurer to a number of questions about his diligence and competence, you ask about the CEO from a negative rather than positive direction. A positive question like "He was competent and diligent, just like you, right?" leaves the door open to a neutral answer: "I really don't know. My boss judged my competence; I didn't judge his."

The negative question, "You have no reason to believe that the CEO was any less competent and diligent than you, right?" invites a simple "No, I don't," confirming the treasurer's positive perception of the CEO's competence, diligence, and probable awareness of the terms of the loan.

Understand and Work with the Whole Story

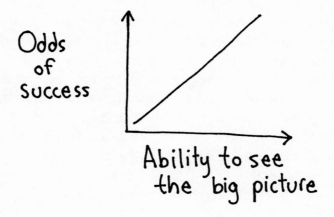

The above sections have explained how to use an indirect approach to cross-examination rather than a frontal attack. Another essential element of strategy is knowing how to work with the whole story of the case. We will again note that this approach closely resembles the strategy used by masters in other types of contests, including on the battlefield.

Know both stories: yours and your adversary's
Sun Tzu advised, "If you know the enemy and know yourself, you need not fear the result of a hundred battles. If you know yourself but not the enemy, for every victory gained you will also suffer a defeat. If you know

neither the enemy nor yourself, you will succumb in every battle."[3]

You like your own case. Your brain is wired by evolution and your competitive instinct to overestimate or dismiss weakness in your case and to underestimate your adversary's strengths. The natural tendency for humans is to fall into Sun Tzu's third category and know neither ourselves nor our enemy. So the use of strategy requires you to look at reality as it is, not as you want it to be, and to understand the positions and strengths and weaknesses from all perspectives. This will give you a three-dimensional perspective in cross-examination and put you in a much better position to anticipate answers of adverse witnesses.

Hedge-fund manager Ray Dalio has gained an advantage in complex and fast-moving markets by understanding the whole, and then making his decisions from that perspective. He calls this "mastering the machine" and conceives of the whole financial system as operating like a complex machine. To make good investment decisions, you proceed from the whole to the specific. This is how Dalio explained it to a New Yorker journalist:

> "Almost everything is like a machine," he told me one day when he was rambling on, as he often does. "Nature is a machine. The family is a machine. The life cycle is like a machine." His constant goal, he said, was to understand how the economic machine works. "And then everything else I basically view as just a case at hand. So how does the machine work that you have a financial crisis? How does deleveraging work — what is the nature of that machine? And

---

[3] Sun Tzu, *The Art of War* (Lexington, KY: SoHo Books, 2010), 20.

what is human nature, and how do you raise a community of people to run a business?"[4]

The trial and its workings are such a machine. If you take a step back and perceive the whole trial machine, you will act much better in each part, particularly in cross-examination.

Even if you have a strong story and a strong case rich in direct evidence, you will have to counter the other side's strengths with indirection, flanking, and attrition by wearing down your adversary. You can only do this by knowing both stories. When I was a prosecutor, my cases had a lot of direct evidence and I often mistook this direct evidence for sufficient strength to win the case on its own. There is greater strength in also accounting for your adversary's story. A story strategist who sees both sides of the story will perceive many more avenues, opportunities, and connections than the lawyer who simply evaluates a case as a winner because the evidence is apparently stronger. Such a strategist will see the positive and negative aspects of many more facts and will be able to convert facts that appear negative on their surface into positive facts.

General Anthony Zinni, a retired four-star Marine Corps general and former commander in chief of the U.S. Central Command, compared a military strategist to a highly experienced quarterback who looks out at the defense as he approaches the line of scrimmage. Zinni noticed that the quarterback doesn't glance back and forth so much as he gazes at the whole field. Zinni did the same on the battlefield and understood that the

---

[4] John Cassidy, "How Ray Dalio Built the World's Richest and Strangest Hedge Fund," *New Yorker*, July 25, 2011, http://www.newyorker.com/magazine/2011/07/25/mastering-the-machine.

quarterback is taking in the whole with one all-encompassing look. The quarterback understands the "story" of the offense and defense together from their current positions. He is able to see how events must unfold in the future from an observation of the present state of things. This is not unlike the so-called "swordsman's gaze" known to martial artists. Merely staring at the opponent's sword—or arm, feet, or torso in the case of the martial arts—is worthless. Looking at all of these together gives a holistic perception and intuitive understanding of the adversary's next move. This kind of perception gives the general, the quarterback, the martial artist, and the trial lawyer the ability to act effectively in a complex situation.[5]

This is why diagramming or mapping out a case—not only chronologically but also in terms of relationships, subjects, and unknowns—rather than making vertical lists is so useful. It allows you to see the whole thing at once rather than individual points one after another. If you have a complete knowledge of the case from the perspective of both sides, you know the points that you want to make and you can relax and pull the questions toward those points without being glued to your prepared questions.

Know your adversary's best story

Amateur chess players are familiar with the anxiety of hoping that your opponent won't see a winning move that will end the game. As an attorney you must be able to anticipate your adversary's best story and build your own story in relation to it, rather than hoping that your opponent won't see certain facts and will construct a weaker story than yours or will fail to call

---

[5] Tom Clancy with General Tony Zinni and Tony Koltz, *Battle Ready* (Berkeley, CA: Berkley Trade, 2005), 53–55.

certain witnesses. What is the strongest story that the opposing side can create, and what is the strongest evidence that supports that story? How will you counter that best story if your opponent makes all the right moves?

Make a story that explains both sides

Trials are conflicts between two fact-based narratives. The more you can co-opt the other side's story by offering a narrative that explains their facts, the stronger you will be because you're refuting their theory without disputing their facts. You're creating a new unified story using the same characters, setting, props, and events that your adversary used. But your story, enriched by your realistic inclusion of the other side's facts, has the depth of truth, common sense, and values that make it come alive in the jury's imagination. Your opponent's story is more one dimensional, constructed around a narrow point of view in the hope that the jury will see it the same way in a leap of faith. When you include the other side's facts in your narrative, you offer the jury a rational alternative based on consideration of the whole picture.

Reverse Chronology

The human brain perceives time as moving in a forward arrow. Stories and narratives are harder to follow, if not outright confusing, if they don't proceed in chronological order. Questioning a witness about events in reverse chronology creates a complex task for the witness in addition to everything else the witness is trying to grapple with. It is difficult under those conditions for witnesses to calculate a deceptive strategy and they may be more forthright in their answers.

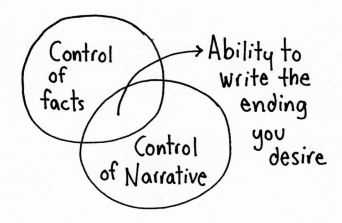

For example, if your goal is to get the witness to admit that event A caused event B, don't ask if event A caused event B. Instead, reverse the order of the events, starting your questioning with event B. Work backward step by step—the smaller the steps the better—asking only about facts and events, never asking the witness to evaluate cause and effect.

When you reverse chronology in this way, you have the line of events mapped out while the witness does not. Even for a sophisticated witness with an agenda, such as a highly paid expert, it's hard to see where the questioning is going when the chronology is reversed. Using reverse chronology in this way gives the jury a feeling of "post hoc ergo proper hoc" (what happened after something happened, happened because of that thing.) The strict rules of logic dictate post hoc non ergo proper hoc, but you can repair any gaps in strict logic elsewhere in your case if you have gotten the witness to admit the factual framework.

In chapter 4 I discussed applying the Greek literary device of hysteron proteron, "putting the other thing first," by writing out your summation during your trial preparation. It can also be used as a reverse chronology technique by stating another, more important thing before the thing that happened first. The classic example is from Virgil's epic poem the *Aeneid*: "Let us die and charge into the midst of the battle." In our example above of the CEO and the loan document the obvious question is, "Did you read the document before you signed it?" Using hysteron proteron, you would start with the signing of the document. This is the most significant act, so your questioning of the CEO would draw out the physical act of signing the document binding his company to a $350 million loan. Then you ask him about what he knew and was told before signing this paper. This approach disrupts the CEO's planned narrative approach of saying he just signed a paper without knowing what was in it. He can still say that, but the claim will not be placed at the end of a long prepared explanation where he wants it. When you have controlled how the narrative is presented by putting the final but more important thing first, you can then ask a series of questions that the CEO wants to answer about his story of how his secretary just put the paper in front of him and he signed it, with the aim of showing how impossible that story is:

Q: You signed here on page 30, right?

A: Yes.

Q: Page 1 has the words "$350 million Credit Financing Agreement," right?

A: Yes, but I didn't see that.

Q: Somebody put it in front of you and you signed it?

A: Yes.

Q: You signed it without reading it?

A: Yes.

Q: And by signing the paper that you didn't read, you borrowed $350 million?

A: Yes.

Q: You put your name under whatever the bank had written in the paper you didn't read?

A: Yes.

Q: The paper that you didn't read also had a guarantee that you didn't read?

A: Yes.

Q: And the guarantee that you didn't read triggered a tax liability?

A: Yes, eventually, but I couldn't have foreseen that.

Q: Couldn't have foreseen it because you did not read the paper with "$350 million Loan" written on the front page?

A: Yes.

By using this reverse chronology approach to the witness's planned story, you have taken control of the battle of the stories about how important and how busy the CEO was and how he delegates everything and relies on his underlings to read everything and he just signs what they give him. Best of all, you have done this by using the very questions he wants to answer about how he never read the $350 million loan agreement, but in your order and context. The CEO has now lost all credibility.

Liddell Hart's Eight Principles

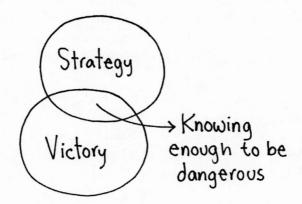

The strategy of winning contests is a set of ideas drawn originally from the methods of battle and war but applied to other fields, as we do here with cross-examination. Over time, I learned or discovered a number of approaches to cross-examination and noted them. It was only when I read Basil Liddell Hart's book *Strategy* that it struck me how the precepts of military strategy could be applied to cross-examination, and how when searching for an original cross-examination or preparing for a difficult witness, a return to Liddel Hart's principles is helpful.

Liddell Hart summarized his military strategies in eight maxims, six positive and two negative.[6] Below I explain how they can be applied to cross-examination.

Positive Principles
1. *"Adjust your ends to your means."*
Choose points for cross-examination that you can win. Understand your case and your adversary's and

---

[6] Liddle Hart, *Strategy*, 334–337.

make a plan that is practical and does not try to accomplish too much. Don't ask questions that allow the witness the option of a bad answer that doesn't benefit your case. Only ask questions to which the witness must give good answers or lose credibility.

2. *"Keep your object always in mind."*

Resist the temptation to engage the witness on paths that stray from your goal. This often happens when the witness gives an arrogant or silly answer that is tempting to pursue but doesn't lead to your point.

3. *"Choose the line (or course) of least expectation."*

In cross-examination, a well-prepared witness will be expecting questions on the strongest parts of your case. There is always a way to approach these points from a perspective that isn't obvious to the witness, from an angle the witness doesn't expect, in order to prevent the witness from immediately understanding the narrative line of your questions and responding with a prepared (lawyer-coached) response.

4. *"Exploit the line of least resistance—so long as it can lead you to any objective which would contribute to your underlying object."*

This is known as flanking, or attacking the least protected positions, in war usually from the side or rear. We have talked about constructing a story along the line of least resistance. Think of questions that the witness will want to answer in a way that's useful to you.

5. *"Take a line of operation which offers alternative objectives. For you will thus put your opponent on the horns of a dilemma which goes far to assure the chance of gaining one objective at least—whichever he guards least—and may enable you to gain one after the other."*

In the vast majority of cross-examinations, you can formulate two alternative goals: one for positive answers, admissions, or concessions, and one for negative answers or denials. This was demonstrated in the "knave or fool" scenario in the civil loan case above. You ask about facts that either force the witness to make an admission or (more likely) make the witness appear like an extreme fool or incompetent.

6. *"Ensure that both plan and dispositions are flexible— adaptable to circumstances."*

In any contest where the adversary can act against you or on equal terms, no rigid plan, list, or outline will prevail throughout the contest. Flexibility and improvisation are at the heart of this book.

Negative Principles

7. *"Do not throw your weight into a stroke whilst your opponent is on guard—whilst he is well placed to parry or evade it."*

This maxim echoes number 3 above, "Choose the line (or course) of least expectation," but emphasizes the timing of a strategy. In order to take the least expected path to your goal, you time important questions so that the significance of the question is not obvious to the witness. This can be hard to do but effective. Ask a question whose point is not obvious, or ask it at a point in the examination that makes it hard for the witness to figure out its purpose.

8. *"Do not renew an attack along the same line (or in the same form) after it has once failed."*

This principle is related to having two goals. If it's clear that the witness will not concede an inch in the first few questions, then there is nothing to be gained by pursuing an admission, especially compared with what you could gain by pursuing an alternative goal, such as showing that a claim of ignorance is impossible.

Cross-examination is a dynamic and competitive activity within a trial that itself changes and adapts as each side makes its moves. Studying and understanding the nature of strategy will make your trial planning better, and using strategic cross-examination as part of your trial plan will make you better still.

A good storyteller understands that the surface of a story does not reveal the depth. In the same way, a good strategist searches for the nonobvious way, the way that the adversary and witness are not prepared to counter—the indirect way. This requires creative thinking and is not amenable to recipes and lists and paint-by-numbers thinking. An important way to engage the creative brain is to look honestly at the whole of the trial so that you can see the strong and weak points of both sides. As you do this you search for ways not obvious at first to make your points on cross-examination and lead your story to its desired ending.

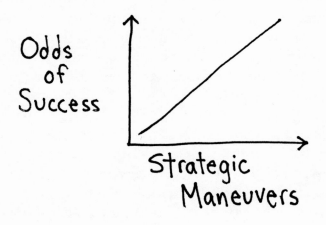

These principles of masterful cross-examination have been studied, tried, and proven in many other fields involving battles between opposing forces. They show that while truth is the ultimate goal of our legal system, simply stating the truth is not enough: a lawyer's superior strategic skill is needed to get judges and juries to see and understand the truth.

CHAPTER SUMMARY

Main Takeaway

A trial is a battle of your story versus your opponent's story that has a winner and a loser. To win this battle you need to effectively use principles of strategy for winning contests. Winning strategies used in a variety of other contests—sports, military campaigns, politics, marketing, and games like chess and cards— can be applied to cross-examination.

Earthquake Points

Use these questions to plan your cross-examination strategy:

- How can I approach my goal indirectly without making it obvious to the witness?

- Can I find ideas outside the law to help me?

- What is the long way around that is really the shortest way there?

- What are my adversary's strengths and weaknesses? What are my own? How do the two fit together?

- How can I arrange facts and questions so as to not reveal the whole of my story?

- What admissions can I gain that the witness won't fight?

- What are the two paths of questioning, the positive and the negative?

- What strategy presents itself by stepping back and viewing the whole?

- How can I plan my questions in reverse chronology or by putting later things first?

- What is the least obvious path?

- How can I use Basil Liddell Hart's eight principles for winning battles to plan my cross-examination?

CHAPTER 8

THE ANSWER AND THE NEXT QUESTION

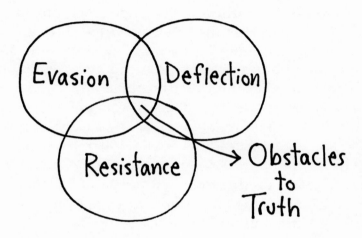

THIS CHAPTER IS ABOUT the actual interchange of cross-examination, the game itself. In the previous chapters you learned how to deeply prepare your case before entering the courtroom. You have the facts at your fingertips and you intend to use them to build your story during your cross-examination of the witness. You now face a different challenge: whereas during your opening statement or summation you're operating alone and are in control of what happens, during cross-examination there is another person, a witness—usually somewhat clever—trying to resist and undo your purpose and the facts you want to present to the jury. The outcome of your cross-examination will depend on your ability to dance fluidly with this witness as you ask questions, field answers, reformulate new questions, and attempt to overcome the witness's resistance as you move the witness closer and closer to the true facts of your story.

Your list of prepared topics may get this dance started, but it's not enough to get you to your end goal. It's just as important to prepare for the witness's answers as it is to prepare the initial questions you're going to ask the witness about a specific topic. But how do you prepare for the answer when you can never be exactly sure how the witness will respond to your cross-examination questions? Fortunately, even though you can't predict the exact response, the range of answers is limited to the facts, arguments, conclusions, and falsities that are inherent in any case. The possible answers to your questions are like the moves in a game of chess: although the moves themselves are complex and you can't predict them with certainty, the pieces on the board are finite and governed by specific rules that you can learn and understand.

The methods that witnesses use to deflect the attention of the judge and jury away from the truth follow predictable patterns of human behavior. It is human nature to seek to bolster our position by choosing—consciously or subconsciously—what part of the truth we convey, how we color that truth, or whether to tell the truth at all. None of us is immune to this human foible, but at trial everything revolves around truth and falsehood and each player applies specific strategies to advance a particular version of the truth. This is the witness's agenda as the witness answers each of your questions, and you need to be able to frame the answer you receive in the context of that agenda and see the methods that are being used to advance it. Then you will be able to turn the witness's methods to your benefit, instead of being caught off guard by an unexpected tactic, or worse, not realizing what's happening and unwittingly handing over control of the cross-examination to the witness.

In this chapter I set out some of the methods that witnesses use to resist giving a truthful answer and present tools that you can use to get past those tactics. If you have a command of the facts, you can use these tools, in combination with your knowledge, instinct, and common sense, to successfully counter a witness's false moves with the truth.

Not all stumbling blocks in cross-examination arise from a witness's evasive tactics, however. No matter how thorough your preparation is, you will most likely miss some facts that only come to light during cross-examination, and there will be turns of events that no one could have predicted. Your deep preparation combined with specific strategies presented here will help you weather those.

Worst-Case Preparation

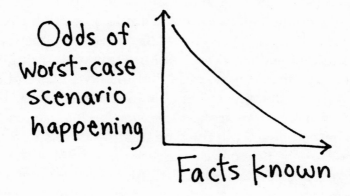

The success of your cross-examination has to lie somewhere between great and horrible. If it's great, the hardest part will be making your exit at the right time (this means sooner rather than later). Great cross-examinations take care of themselves, so why not spend most of your time preparing for the most difficult scenario?

One key to preparing for the worst possibility is to have a deep understanding not only of your own case, but of your opponent's case. Many lawyers don't want to hear the other side's best case and facts, or dismiss them as irrelevant. It's psychologically hard to shift your focus to the other side's case, especially for competitive lawyers. It can be time consuming to write out your opponent's arguments and facts, but this is time well spent: if you can figure out how to deal with the other side's most powerful facts and arguments and carefully think about the worst possible answer a witness can give you on cross-examination, you give yourself the advantage over lawyers who have only been thinking about their own position.

So really, what is the worst thing a witness can say to you on cross-examination? It is to state a true fact that you either didn't know or didn't understand. This is when you're hurt the most. The next most damaging is when the witness gives an answer that puts a fact into a bigger context than you had understood before. For example, you get the witness to acknowledge that he was fired by his last boss, thinking this will impugn his credibility. But then he adds that his boss was indicted on extortion charges and is now in federal prison, a fact that you weren't aware of.

These answers are the true turning points of a case. Spend time trying to imagine these potential situations. Find the possible crises and think about your reaction to them. Some possible responses include remaining calm to convey that you aren't taken by surprise; treating the topic as unimportant; letting go of a line of questioning if you can't find an advantageous way through it and going on to another topic; or simply stopping your cross-examination.

Don't just think through the worst-case scenario. Visualize it physically and imagine yourself trying to escape from it. French Canadian martial arts champion Georges St-Pierre used this technique to prepare to fight Matt Serra, a master wrestler. Once Serra had an opponent on the ground he was nearly unstoppable at pinning him or obtaining his submission. St-Pierre said that he devoted a large part of his training to starting from the position of being within inches of being pinned and trying to escape. When you train in this way, you force your mind to think up more powerful creative solutions and you conquer your fear.

If you have prepared deeply and internalized your facts and your story strategy as well as those of your adversary, you will be ready—instinctively, without a lot of thinking—to respond with the best questions in any situation, even if the situation is not one you had anticipated. Just as in a game of chess, you have a deep understanding of all of the elements of the case, both those that are in your favor and those that are not, and you have a clear vision of your end goal. Then you let your instinct do the rest and guide you through the sticking points in the courtroom.

Prepare for Story Counterstrategy

What is your opponent's stated counterstrategy? By the time you're actually cross-examining you certainly know your adversaries' theory of the case and the facts that they argue are important to their theory. But the time you spend reading briefs, complaints, and answers and going over transcripts of pretrial arguments to see how the other side fits facts to arguments will pay off by helping you anticipate how their witnesses will answer your questions. Remember, the other side is also trying to construct a factually strong and well-argued case, so everything you can find out to understand how they're doing that will help you on cross-examination.

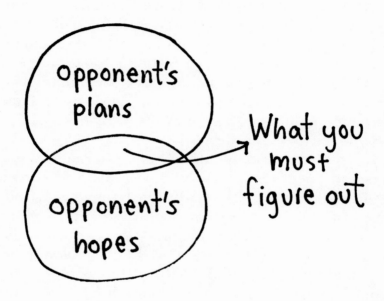

What answers given by your opponent's witness will best get their story out? Expand your search beyond what the other side has already stated in the case to all the additional facts that you know. How will the witness put these facts together in the most effective way to harm your case and help theirs? Once you have identified the worst possible answers you can separate them into valid and invalid responses. Valid answers are truthful and provide legitimate inferences that work against your case. Invalid answers are cheats in some way: they involve some type of distortion, evasion, and so on to advance the other party's position. What kind of invalid answers can you expect?

Prepare for Getting the Truth from Your Witness

"He's a walking contradiction, partly truth and partly fiction," sings Kris Kristofferson in "The Pilgrim, Chapter 33." He might have been referring to some trial witnesses.

Your goal is to get truthful answers from your witness. One way to put the odds of doing that in your favor is to ask questions that the witness will most likely answer truthfully. There are always a number of facts that both sides agree on, or that witnesses think are helpful to their case but in fact are more helpful to yours. Questions having to do with these kinds of facts are more likely to get truthful answers than questions seeking facts that are obviously harmful to your adversary's case. Questions about facts that are backed by hard-to-refute evidence that the witness is aware of will also generally produce truthful answers.

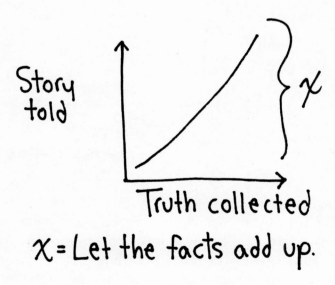

X = Let the facts add up.

You ask a simple question and the witness gives you a direct, truthful answer. Great. No need to prepare for that, right? Wrong. Getting a truthful answer is like winning money at a casino—you're likely to lose it if you're not careful. Ultimately, the best way to prepare for a truthful answer is to prepare to leave it. Learn to recognize a truthful answer when you get it, and immediately move on to a new topic. It can be tempting to pursue the question further, but like Odysseus trying to resist the lure of the Sirens by having his crew tie him to the mast of his ship, you must sail by the temptation to emphasize, repeat, amplify, or follow through on the implications of a truthful answer.

Contradiction

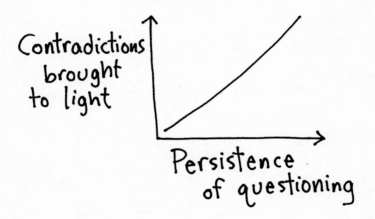

Like finding the truth, it is not as easy to prepare to uncover contradictions in a witness's testimony as you might think. That's because when you're on your feet cross-examining, testimony often seems more contradictory than it really is—you may think you're doing better at ferreting out inconsistencies than you actually are. Like most people who are trying to support a specific point or goal, lawyers tend to hear what they want to hear. You may think you're developing a clear picture of a witness's contradictory statement, while the judge and jury aren't seeing it. You need to project confidence, but don't let your confidence delude you into automatically thinking that your points are clear.

In my experience, unless you plan to confront the witness squarely and specifically, you will not be able to reveal a contradiction. The way to plan for this is to figure out what documents or prior statements are likely to be contradicted by the witness and then use the exact words of those documents in your questions. If you use approximate or similar language, your adversary and perhaps the judge will say the statement is not inconsistent.

If you have reduced your case to its atomic facts, some of those will be factual statements made by the witness prior to trial. Anything longer than a simple sentence is of no use as a contradiction. You should discard, for the purpose of showing contradiction, all other statements. When you are selecting prior statements made by a witness that you hope to use to contradict that witness, don't use long statements, opinions, or vague or nonfactual statements. That will generally not go well. Out of ten statements a witness has made in the past, only one may be useful for contradicting the witness.

Omission

It's human nature for witnesses to omit facts that weaken the point they want to make. It may not be deliberate—people have a tendency to forget things that undermine their goal or argument as they focus on the things that support their goals. The nature of testimony is to draw on memories to create a narrative. A fact that doesn't fit into the witness's narrative will get left out.

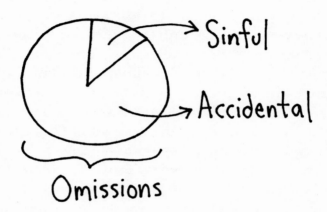

The first step in preparing to deal with an omission is to understand what is happening. If the omission is not intentional, refrain from attacking the witness as a liar. As you listen to the testimony, you must not only listen for what is there but also for what is not there. You need to train yourself to do this kind of listening.

When witnesses omit a fact, ask if they have left anything out. Most of the time they will say no, in which case you simply ask, "In your testimony you didn't mention fact X, did you?" Then stop. During your final argument you can explain to the jury how fact X, if included, would undermine the witness's entire narrative.

If the witness answers yes, say, "You left out fact X on your direct examination? You didn't mention it?" Then your next series of questions should point out how fact X could change the significance of the narrative that the witness was putting forth in direct examination.

Evasion

Evasion is by far the most common way for an adversarial witness to respond. Often you will spend an entire cross-examination trying to pin down a witness on just one fact. This is why restricting yourself to key facts is important.

The first step to prepare for evasion is to expect it. Witnesses evade because they think a direct, truthful answer will be harmful to their side of the case. The second step is to know exactly what the true answer to your question is. Third, make your question simple and clear so that it calls for that answer and only that answer.

Evasion can take many forms. If you can recognize and identify the tactics the witness is using to avoid answering the factual question you have asked, you can respond to the evasion. Sometimes the best strategy is to simply identify the evasive answer and point out to the jury what the witness is doing.

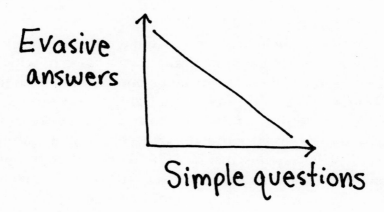

You can expect the following forms of evasion when you cross-examine a sophisticated witness such as a corporate executive, government agent, or professional expert witness.

"I don't remember"

The most common form of evasion is when witnesses claim that they don't remember a fact. This could be true or not true, depending on three factors: the importance of the fact, how long ago it happened, and whether the fact is good or bad for the witness's side of the case.

The best way to prepare for "I don't remember" is to have ready as many facts as you can that relate to the fact you're asking about. If the fact that the witness claims to not remember is significant, happened recently enough to be within normal memory, and is bad for the side the witness represents, then lack of memory is probably false. You can use the surrounding facts to compare the fact that the witness "forgot" with less important facts, more recent facts, and facts that are good for the witness's side, all of which the witness does remember.

"I don't know"

A close cousin to "I don't remember," the "CEO defense" gets its name from the many cases in which, for years, the CEO gets enormous bonuses and millions of dollars in stock options from the reported profits of the corporation. Then, when those profit reports turn out to have been false because of accounting manipulation, the CEO testifies that he didn't know enough about accounting to realize that those reports were fraudulent.

When witnesses claim to not know something that should be within their sphere of knowledge, or from which they gained something, pointing out the benefits of this ignorance, including escaping liability, is an effective way to cross-examine. The best facts to have ready are documents or statements in which the witness talked about the numbers or profits and in which the witness used accounting terms in conference calls or other communications to convince the public that the company's stock was a good investment. Point out the benefits that the witness got from not knowing the accounting was false, and that if the jury accepts this claim of not knowing (thus finding the witness lacking the intent needed to prove liability), the witness will have gotten rich not by talent but by ignorance. By setting up a contrast between what witnesses do know and remember and what they claim they don't, you can show the implausibility of this ignorance.

Filibuster

Witnesses who have the ability to talk on and on will evade questions by giving you a three-minute answer to a three-second question. This technique buries the answer they don't want to give in mounds of self-serving context, or often just gives a large number of words that don't answer the question at all.

The standard response to a filibuster is to say, "You've given me a long answer to a short question. My question was simply whether fact X is true. Is it true or not?" With this witness, you must be careful to frame your questions so that they can only be answered with "yes" or "no." This means they must be extremely short, usually not even a complete sentence. The more the witness talks, the shorter you make your questions, so that you can make clear what the witness is doing and support your demand for a yes or no answer.

Answering the other question

This is how politicians answer questions to divert attention away from something they would rather avoid. Politicians don't have a judge hovering over them to make them answer questions, but you as a cross-examiner have that power, supported by the judge. The method for dealing with this is similar to the filibuster. Repeat your original question by saying, "Perhaps I wasn't clear. This is my question." If the witness continues to evade, you persist: "Perhaps you didn't understand the question. This is the question."

Giving opinions instead of facts

Responding to a question that asks for a fact by giving an inference, opinion, or conclusion is another common way to evade the question. You have removed opinions and conclusions from your own case by reducing it to atoms, so you should be able to recognize when a witness is putting up opinion as fact.

Often witnesses testify directly and clearly on direct examination and give factual testimony. On cross-examination, however, the same witnesses may try to slip in opinions and inferences favorable to their side. They might also give inferences in favor of their case on direct and then claim ignorance of those inferences that undermine their case on cross-examination.

Witnesses who do this will often answer your questions by claiming that the question calls for speculation, when they have just provided speculation in favor of their case. Simply pointing out prior statements of opinion is an effective way to cross-examine these witnesses. Ask questions like "This is a fact, right?" And then, "Your earlier answer is something you believe, not what you saw, heard, or felt, right?" But as with all evasion, it is best to go all the way to ground by asking the simplest, even physical factual questions.

Spin

Evasion can also take the form of "spin." This is when a witness has a canned or prepared explanation, like the talking points that politicians use, for a document or prior statement that attempts to change the original meaning of the statement. Talking points are a common way for witnesses to prepare for cross-examination.

You should cross-examine spin by getting under it to the plain words of the prior statement. Take them apart so that the contrast between the simple words of the document or statement contrast vividly with the spin the witness is trying to pull off.

Lies

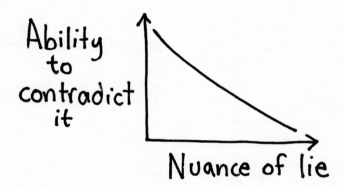

It is not common for a witness to lie outright. Most lies told by witnesses are subtle or shaded because they know that larger lies will be easily detected and cast doubt on their character and testimony. Witnesses won't lie more than they need to: if they only need to exaggerate or omit something they will do that instead of lying. It can be shocking when a witness tells an obvious lie, and you should prepare for the possibility.

The most common type of lie is exaggeration, which is obviously a matter of degree. It can be a little or a lot. Be ready. If you have a document or hard evidence that contradicts the lie, that's ideal. But it's also rare. Witnesses most often choose to lie about things that are hard to contradict.

Your first response should be to push the witness further in the direction of the lie. That is, if they exaggerate, get them to exaggerate even more. If it's an outright lie, get the witness to confirm it, and perhaps state other, related lies. By pushing the liar to further the lie, you are both weakening the witness's credibility—at some point it just becomes unbelievable—and widening the scope of the lie. Most good lies are crafted so that they cannot be directly contradicted. But as the lie expands the liar may unwittingly take it into an area that you can objectively contradict with other evidence.

This way, even if you don't have at hand the means to contradict the specific lie in the moment, you have increased your probability of being able to contradict the witness with other evidence. You have also increased your probability of convincing the jury that the witness's testimony is implausible. Remember that there is a spectrum of answers, from a simple admission of truth (equaling credibility) to the most implausible answer that destroys a witness's credibility.

Prepare the Next Question

For each kind of witness answer described above, there are particular tactics that you can use in your follow-up question. This is like reaching into a toolbox and selecting the right tool for the job. The process is improvisational, so these tools are easy-to-remember guidelines rather than hard rules.

The Flashlight: Identify what is happening
The first thing you need to do is to identify what the

witness is doing and shine a light on it. Is the witness lying, telling the truth, exaggerating? Those are easy. Harder to identify are the shades of evasion, like substituting opinion for fact or spinning. Think in advance about these witness tactics and plan to pause for a few seconds, breathe, and mentally identify exactly what the witness is doing.

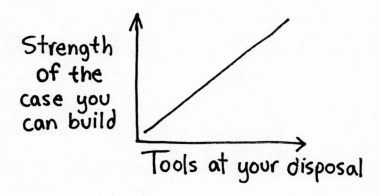

Strength of the case you can build

Tools at your disposal

The Ladder: Climb your way up to the real answer

When a witness gives an answer that doesn't really answer your question, use a ladder to get to the true answer. Each rung on the ladder is the same, and so your question should be the same, but with each repetition, you go to a higher level.

Lowest rung: Simply repeat the question in an even tone.

Next rung: Play nice, saying, "Perhaps I wasn't clear." Repeat the exact same question.

Next rung: "Maybe you didn't understand me." Repeat the same question.

Next rung: "Mr. Witness, you answered X, but the question is . . . " Repeat the question and ask, "Is X really your answer to that question?"

If at this point the witness persists in not answering your question, then you have done all you could, short of a judge intervening, to show that the witness has substituted a personal talking point for the real answer to the question. You can now move on and in your summation answer the question yourself and explain to the jury that the witness avoided answering the question because it was bad for him or her, and that the witness should not be believed.

The Hammer: Pound with facts

The key to all cross-examination is to start with a fact. Facts are grounded and they give you power and leverage because they have weight, as opposed to opinions or conclusions. Hit the witness with facts again and again, as if you're swinging a hammer. If the witness gives an opinion, you ask, "Fact X is true, right?" "Your last statement goes beyond fact X, doesn't it?" "Your last statement suggests an inference that you've made from fact X, correct?"

When you're trying to get a witness to agree with you it's always better to suggest the answer in a complimentary rather than accusatory way. Don't use words like "speculation" or "just your personal opinion." You're more likely to get witnesses to agree that they have made an inference than that they are speculating or giving an opinion. Being ready to ask about fact after fact is the best way to cross-examine a witness who is trying to get away with presenting an opinion disguised as fact.

Thumbtacks: Small and many

When a witness claims lack of knowledge or memory that you think is feigned, ask about a number of small surrounding or related facts that the witness will agree to, gradually pinning the witness to the truth with these smaller "thumbtacks." Feigned lack of memory or knowledge usually means that witnesses remember what is good for them but forget what is bad, and using small facts and pairing what they remember and forget is an effective tactic.

The Saw: Cut it apart

Most suspect testimony comes in longer answers that bundle a number of facts. The same statement could contain fact, a lie, and an opinion, and as a whole be an evasive statement. You have to have the patience to take apart such answers and ask a series of questions that, piece by piece, point out what is true, what is not, what is exaggerated, and what is speculation. This can take a long time, and often you can make only one point on cross-examination if there is a limit to your time.

Sandpaper: Take off the edges

When testimony is not outright false you can effectively cross-examine by getting witnesses to concede points that are not at the core of their testimony. You can take a lot of negative impact away from the witness's testimony by accumulating a number of small concessions that the witness did not perceive, somehow exaggerated, spun, or was not 100 percent certain of. A list of these kinds of concessions is effective when you present it to a jury on summation.

The Ax: Walk away and be seated

Walking away and sitting down allows you to either survive bad testimony or preserve good testimony. Cut

205

things off in the most graceful way you can, either by changing the subject or by asking a few other questions and then sitting down. Do this not only when you're surprised by something bad that you can't deal with immediately, but also after you have gained good testimony that will be hard to improve on. Failing to walk away or stop questioning at the right time can turn good testimony into bad and bad testimony into disaster. You can usually repair or lessen the damages with other witnesses or evidence and on summation.

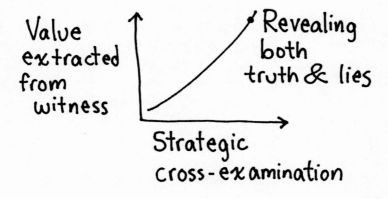

CHAPTER SUMMARY

Main Takeaway

Preparing for the witness's answers to your questions is just as important as the initial questions themselves. Witnesses use several predictable methods to avoid telling the truth. If you recognize these strategies you can use a number of tools to counter them and get the truth out while exposing the witness's deception.

Earthquake Points

- Witnesses use predictable strategies to resist answering your questions truthfully. If you know what these strategies are you can prepare for and counter them.

- Prepare for the worst-case answer by having a deep understanding of your case and your opponent's and by planning how you will deal with the most damaging answers.

Ways to counter witnesses' deception strategies

- Ask questions that the witness will most likely answer truthfully: questions about facts that both sides agree on, facts that the witness thinks are in the witness's favor, and evidence that can't be reasonably refuted.

- When you get a truthful answer move on to something else. Otherwise you risk the witness undoing it somehow.

- Predict what documents and previous statements are likely to be contradicted by the witness and use the exact words of those documents and statements in your questions to expose contradictions.

- Listen for omissions in the witness's answers. Then ask questions that show how the omitted fact changes the witness's story.

- If the witness claims to not remember a fact, ask about the surrounding facts.

- Counter long, evasive answers with short, pointed questions.

- Repeat questions to get a truthful answer from an evasive witness.

- Get witnesses to admit when they're giving opinions or drawing inferences.

- Push witnesses who lie further toward the lie to damage their credibility.

Tools for follow-up questions

The Flashlight: Identify the witness's evasive strategy.

The Ladder: Rephrase questions with increasing pressure on the evasive witness.

The Hammer: Hit the witness repeatedly with facts.

Thumbtacks: Pin the witness to the truth with several small facts related to the fact the witness is trying to avoid.

The Saw: Cut apart a long answer to show which parts are truth, exaggeration, or speculation.

Sandpaper: Get the witness to concede a number of surrounding facts to weaken the central point.

The Ax: To end damaging testimony or preserve helpful testimony, either change the topic or walk away and sit down.

Part 3

LIFE-LONG

MASTERY

CHAPTER 9

FLUID THINKING AND MIND-BODY

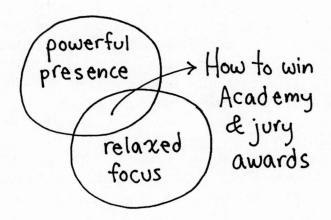

Nᴇᴡ Yᴏʀᴋ Yᴀɴᴋᴇᴇꜱ ᴄᴀᴛᴄʜᴇʀ Yᴏɢɪ Bᴇʀʀᴀ knew baseball and he knew life. Yogi once said, "The game is ninety percent mental. The other half is physical." Lawyers usually think of cross-examination—in fact the whole business of lawyering—as an exclusively mental process. But cross-examination is in fact a mind-body activity. If Yogi were a lawyer he would have said, "Cross-examination is ninety percent physical. The other half is mental."

What happens in the courtroom has a strong physical component that has a distinct impact—for better or for worse—on the outcome of the trial contest between you and your adversary. This physical component consists of your awareness and conscious use of such things as your inner state of tension or calm, heart rate, energy, modulation of your voice and how quickly you speak, your body language, and your movements about the courtroom.

A lawyer who cross-examines with physical presence and physical confidence thinks better, listens better, and gets to the truth better. Moreover, such a lawyer is more persuasive, in part due to enhanced credibility and authority consistent with Aristotle's *ethos*, the first element of persuasion.[1] Humans are highly visual, and the judge and jury are watching your every move and perceiving the conscious or unconscious signals that you give off that tell them about your skill, confidence, intelligence, and sincerity, which they equate with your credibility.

In order to present a persuasive cross-examination, you need to have optimal speaking and listening skills. Here too, physical awareness is essential. If you are in control of your body—your breathing, your posture, and so on—you will speak more slowly, in a more resonant voice, both of which have been found to enhance credibility.[2] Listening too depends on being in a calm yet attentive physical state. Physical awareness puts you in the relaxed, perceptive state that allows your brain to process what it is actually seeing rather than being focused on notes or papers and trying to predict what might happen next. You "see" the witness, the

---

[1] Aristotle's *On Rhetoric*, Book II, describes three bases of persuasion for public speaking: *ethos* (credibility), *pathos* (the audience's emotion), and *logos* (reasoning).

[2] Norman Miller, Geoffrey Maruyama, Rex Julian Beaber, and Keith Valone, "Speed of Speech and Persuasion, *Journal of Personality and Social Psychology* 34, no. 4 (1976): 615–624.

judge, and the jury better and pick up more information about their reactions to your cross-examination. All of these benefits will increase your ability to ask the best cross-examination questions, ones that are just right for the situation and that flow from what has just happened to where you want to go.

The idea of a strong physical component to cross-examination and trial preparation and strategy is subversive to lawyers and to the law-firm profit model of billing for sitting long hours in a chair reading papers. The very concept that you could prepare to do better cross-examination by walking, yoga, and physical exercise is thought of as frivolous and work avoiding. But writer and educator George Leonard, who investigated ways to enhance human potential by combining physical, mental, and spiritual strategies, reminds us to prepare mentally for a physical test and prepare physically for a mental test. The mind and body are inseparable and both need to be in excellent working order. The lawyer who cultivates mind and body and employs them together in daily life and legal practice has a competitive advantage in cross-examination and at trial generally. In this chapter you will learn how to prepare both mentally and physically for the rapid dynamics of cross-examination.

Fluid Thinking

The mind-body connection supports *fluid thinking*, an intuitive process that can be used to make quick decisions in novel situations in the constantly changing environment of the courtroom. Lawyers do not normally train for or practice fluid thinking. The combination of your awareness and use of physical processes with fluid thinking will greatly improve your efforts to find and lucidly present the truth in your case. Fluid thinking is used in a wide variety of activities involving both the mind and the body, along a spectrum from the mostly physical, such as fighting sports, football, and baseball, to commonly understood mind-body exercises like yoga and tai chi, as well as activities like musical performance, acting, and cross-examination, whose physical component is not fully appreciated by those who don't practice them.

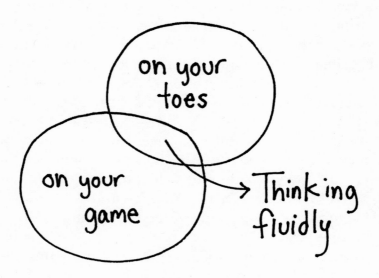

There are three kinds of thinking: analytical, critical, and fluid thinking. Law school teaches static analytical thinking. In law school, you analyze the texts of judges (often dead), and then your professor questions you about the conclusions you draw from these texts and cases. You learn abstract concepts like *intent* and *proximate cause* and reflect on how facts and factors fit into these concepts. This type of thinking is usually quiet and unhurried, and above all logical. Analytical thinking is the kind of thinking that we use to take tests and to argue logically, what is often referred to as "left brain thinking" (although recent science suggests that it may not actually take place in the left brain).[3] It is linear and deals with evaluating facts that are given or static.

Lawyers have to be good at analytical thinking, but as discussed many times in this book, it is not the best mode of thinking for cross-examination because it is too abstract and not perceptual enough. It is a deliberate, methodical mode of thinking that can't keep pace with the rapid turn of events in the courtroom. This type of thinking has a variable relation to the truth because it is not designed for the sole purpose of finding the truth — it is designed for winning arguments and solving abstract problems that may or may not apply to the real world.

Critical thinking is a good tool for seeing the truth, but not so useful for cross-examination because you can get bogged down in identifying the details of a flawed argument, rather than intuitively striking at its heart. Critical thinking means being able to figure out what is wrong with a set of facts, story, theory, or hypothesis, whether it's someone else's (your adversary's) or especially, your own. It is, most importantly, the ability to figure out what is wrong with your own thinking and avoid misjudgments that often come from bias or wrong instincts. Critical thinking is indispensable in your preparation and to making sure that the story you're pursuing really embodies the truth. But it is by definition judgmental and hesitant. It doesn't flow in the moment and isn't designed for thinking on your feet as new or problematic events come up. Focusing only on what is wrong with something isn't enough to open the way to the whole truth.

---

[3] Stephen M. Kosslyn and G. Wayne Miller, "There Is No Left Brain/Right Brain Divide," *Time Magazine*, November 29, 2013.

In analytical thinking, you're a detached observer, after the event has happened. Critical thinking helps you prepare your case and avoid traps and pitfalls that come from being too gullible or hopeful that things will go well. But fluid thinking is for real-time action, when you are a player in a high-stakes game and are at risk.

Fluid thinking, according to John Medina, a molecular biologist and founder of the Brain Center for Applied Learning Research at Seattle Pacific University, is "the ability to reason quickly, and think abstractly, improvising off previously learned material in order to solve a new problem."[4] Sounds to me like exactly the kind of thinking that an effective cross-examiner needs.

The Evolutionary Basis of Fluid Thinking

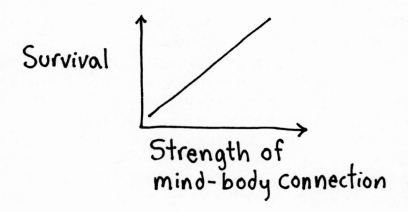

Fluid thinking is a natural process deeply embedded in the human brain, inherited from our primeval ancestors. While it may sound foreign to you simply because your education put value on other types of

---

[4] John Medina, *Brain Rules: 12 Principles for Surviving and Thriving at Work, Home, and School* (Seattle: Pear Press, 2008), 14.

thinking, it is part of your human makeup and therefore it can be activated in service to your goals as a lawyer.

What we seek as cross-examiners is instinctual, rapid recognition of what is happening and the ability to react quickly and choose the best action in every situation. This is what all animals need for survival in their changing environments. Flexibility is at the heart of adaptation for survival. Consider for example what happened during the Ice Age, when humans who had been living in tropical forests had to adapt fairly quickly to a vastly changed water and food supply. The work of paleoanthropologist Richard Potts, director of the Human Origins Program at the Smithsonian's National Museum for Natural History, explains how we came to not only survive those changing conditions but to expand our population around the globe. Pott's theory of variability selection[5] maintains that our ancestors who were adaptable, flexible, and improvisational survived. Those who were inflexible or could not react quickly enough did not. Medina, citing Potts, explains, "You give up on stability. You don't try to beat back the changes. You begin not to care about consistency within a given habitat, because consistency wasn't an option. You adapt to variation itself. . . . Those unable to rapidly solve new problems or learn from mistakes didn't survive long enough to pass on their genes. The net effect of this evolution was that rather than becoming stronger, we became smarter."[6] The importance of rapid adaptation for survival is evident once again in the current global-warming crisis.

Adaptability to changing conditions is the lawyer's key to survival as well. Fortunately, your brain as well

---

[5] Richard Potts, *Humanity's Descent: The Consequences of Ecological Instability* (New York: William Morrow, 1996).

[6] Medina, *Brain Rules*, 37.

217

as your jurors' brains have evolved to think in exactly this way. Effective cross-examination is much closer to the natural and most efficient mode of thinking than the analytical, book-based Socratic thinking that was drummed into your brain in law school.

The closer you keep to natural modes of thinking, the easier and more instinctual your thinking will be, and the more your presentation will naturally appeal to the judges and jurors you want to persuade.

The Physical Basis of Fluid Thinking

We are first and foremost animals who evolved in a hostile environment that constantly challenged our survival. In order to meet their basic survival needs for food, clothing, shelter, and safety, early humans needed to be constantly on the move physically as well as mentally attentive to danger signals and opportunities. Our bodies and brains evolved to work and think physically—our early ancestors walked or ran an average of twelve miles a day.[7] The physicality of thinking stems from the brain's deep evolutionary roots and the purpose of human intelligence: survival. The brain evolved to facilitate optimal physical actions in survival situations. These situations did not happen when cave dwellers were sitting at their desks reading briefs. They happened when they were on their feet, moving rapidly from place to place seeking prey or avoiding becoming prey. Medina sums it up: "The brain appears to be designed to (1) solve problems (2) related to surviving (3) in an unstable outdoor environment, and (4) to do so in nearly constant motion."[8] This very much describes the environment of cross-examination. Our survival as lawyers is winning contests by solving problems in an unstable environment that requires us to move constantly. We can do this best by using our brain the way it was designed to work.

Medina's book *Brain Rules: 12 Principles for Surviving and Thriving at Work, Home, and School* proposes twelve rules on the following page, many of which emphasize the physical nature of thinking.[9]

Medina's brain rules give powerful insights into many aspects of trial practice. Rules 1, 2, 4, 7, 8, 9, 10, and 12 relate directly to the physical roots of thinking. It is well known that exercise is good for you on many levels, but Medina notes that exercisers score higher on tests of fluid thinking and that fluid thinking is particularly harmed by a sedentary lifestyle, like sitting at a desk or a computer, being paid based on the number of hours you can do that, and reading and writing for twelve hours or more a day. We lawyers think this is the

---

[7] Ibid., 23.

[8] Ibid., 32.

[9] This version of the twelve rules is taken from Medina's website, http://brainrules.net/about-brain-rules.

MEDINA'S BRAIN RULES

1.	**Exercise**	Exercise boosts brain power.
2.	**Survival**	The human brain evolved to survive.
3.	**Wiring**	Every brain is wired differently.
4.	**Attention**	We don't pay attention to boring things.
5.	**Short-term memory**	Repeat to remember.
6.	**Long-term memory**	Remember to repeat.
7.	**Sleep**	Sleep well, think well.
8.	**Stress**	Stressed brains don't learn the same way as non-stressed brains.
9.	**Sensory integration**	Stimulate more of the senses.
10.	**Vision**	Vision trumps all other senses.
11.	**Gender**	Male and female brains are different.
12.	**Exploration**	We are powerful and natural explorers.

way to get smarter, but for the kind of fluid thinking that is the core of cross-examination, it is actually making us less smart. Exercise improves the brain's supply of one of the things it needs most to function: oxygen. Exercise is analogous to creating an interstate highway system for the brain.

To better understand how our ancestors' brains are related to what lawyers do today, we return to the most important goal of our legal system: to discover the truth. "Truth" and "reality" are synonymous in this case, and our ancestors needed to be acutely aware of the reality of their environment. The fluid thinking that Medina describes evolved for survival as a means for *discovering the truth*. You will not long survive if your "theory of the case" is that there is an antelope behind a bush when in fact it's a saber-toothed tiger. Survival meant identifying the truth and acting on it correctly, and this is just as true for cross-examiners today.

So trials and cross-examination, far from being unnatural environments, are a natural outgrowth of the human thinking and surviving process. "But wait," you say, "I'm not good at this kind of rapid decision making and quick thinking. I have to analyze something in detail before I act on it. That's why I became a lawyer." In fact you were human before you became a lawyer, and you can relearn the fluid thinking that ensured the survival of early humans and that we still carry in our brains.

Flow and Thinking

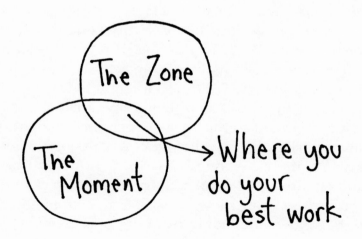

Fluid thinking is a high-level mode of thinking, at the top of the thinking pyramid in that it yields important benefits that are not available to the cross-examiner who relies only on analytical thinking. First and foremost, fluid thinking is a mind-body state characterized by engagement of the whole person and several of the multiple human intelligences, such as listening ability, proprioception (the ability to sense the position and movement of your own body), and physical, spatial, visual, and emotional intelligence.

A primary characteristic of fluid thinking is *presence*, which for the lawyer manifests outwardly as physical comfort in speaking, good posture, and a smooth and relaxed way of listening and responding with the right words in the proper tone. The quality of your courtroom presence is quite important as it sends subconscious messages to your listeners about your confidence, sincerity, motives, and credibility. These qualities come from a feeling that you can handle whatever comes up, rather than relying on a prepared presentation.

The state of presence of fluid thinking is similar to the *flow* described by psychologist Mihaly Csikszentmihalyi in his book *Flow: The Psychology of Optimal Experience*,[10] also known as "being in the zone" or "being in the moment." He briefly defines flow as "the state in which people are so involved in an activity that nothing else seems to matter."[11] Flow is integral to the "optimal experiences" that Csikszentmihalyi says are essential for happiness, similar to the "peak experiences" identified decades earlier by psychologist Abraham Maslow.[12] Csikszentmihalyi further described flow as "being completely involved in an activity for its own sake. The ego falls away. Time flies. Every action, movement, and thought follows inevitably from the previous one, like playing jazz. Your whole being is involved, and you're using your skills to the utmost."[13]

---

[10] New York: Harper Perennial Modern Classics, 2008.

[11] Ibid., 4.

[12] Abraham Maslow, *Religions, Values, and Peak Experiences* (London: Penguin Books, 1964).

In this state you're absorbed in what you're doing, unaware of anything that isn't important to the activity at hand. In these moments you're able to tap into your highest skills and each action flows easily from the one before it. You have a heightened sense of awareness and intuition that allows you to immediately see what you need to do next, even if events diverge from your plan. You feel challenged by the situation, yet confident that you're up to the challenge.

Some of Csikszentmihalyi's data came from his study of artists, athletes, musicians, chess masters, and surgeons—people who need to perform at the highest level of their capacities, with high awareness of what is happening at each moment, and react immediately to each new situation that arises. There is no time to analyze the situation in depth and weigh options. The best course of action needs to flow automatically from the situation. Although these individuals are engaged in activities with very high stakes and are sometimes in competition with others who are highly motivated to win a contest, they have a feeling of calm confidence, even enjoyment of being challenged at this level.

Clearly this is the optimal physical and mental state for the cross-examiner, compared to the high level of stress, anxiety, self-doubt, and confusion that many feel in the courtroom.

How to Develop the Mind-Body Connection and Fluid Thinking

Fluid thinking is not simply a skill that consists of a number of subskills that can be learned one by one. It

---

[13] John Geirland, "Go with the Flow," *Wired*, n.d., http://archive.wired.com/wired/archive/4.09/czik_pr.html.

is more a way of being that permeates different aspects of your life and facets of your personality, which then carry over into the courtroom. You can't learn this kind of thinking from law-school books. You develop it through integrating mind-body practices into your personal and working life and engaging in the type of optimal experiences described above to activate the mind and body.

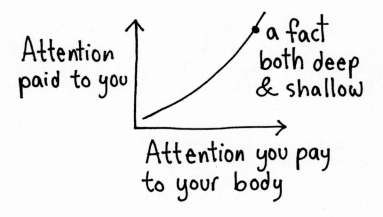

Practice body and mind working together

Engaging the mind and body together and awakening the natural process of fluid thinking starts with physical health and fitness and body awareness. The importance of the mind-body connection and mind-body exercise for health and performance is well known. Mental and physical fitness and flexibility go together and are important for optimal performance in the courtroom.

Exercise needs to be chosen wisely. As an inveterate exerciser I can tell you that I saw no close connection between exercise and improved thinking in the courtroom until I began to exercise my mind fully. I stopped lifting weights and going to the gym and switched to exercises that required me to concentrate and put my full mind into exactly what my body was doing. I began studying martial arts and boxing. I took fencing lessons. I took swimming lessons from Terry Laughlin, whose Total Immersion program embodies mindful concentration on form and performance of motion. I now use kettlebells and progressive calisthenics, which emphasize relaxation with a tight core and loose limbs and unity of mind and body.

Ralph La Forge, an exercise physiologist at Duke University Medical Center, describes the common features of mindful exercise.[14] First, it is "mentative" and introspective, focusing on the *present moment* and the *process of the activity*. Second, it places attention on *muscles and movement, breathing, proper physical form,* and *energy flow*. Those qualities, La Forge says, are found in exercises like yoga, tai chi, qigong, pilates, and certain forms of dance. I also recommend competitive sports such as boxing, martial arts, fencing, tennis, and even ping pong, which all require a high degree of fluid thinking. In sports like these you must be intensely present in the moment with heightened physical and mental awareness in order to perceive what your adversary is doing, and then, with only a split second to think, act in the right way.

Sometimes your action is a response and sometimes it's part of your own overall plan. The point is that these kinds of sports for fun and exercise are supportive of fluid thinking, much more so than physical activities like jogging or working on an elliptical machine, where your mind is not needed. In boxing or fencing, your mind needs to be aware and alert

---

[14] Ralph La Forge, "The Art and Science of Mind-Body Exercise in Health & Disease," spot.pcc.edu/~lkidoguc/PAMBD/TR03_ArtScience.pdf.

while you're moving and expending effort. If you're not alert in these sports, you will get punched or stuck with a rapier. These rapid responses and decisions don't come from analytical thinking, and these examples show why analytical thinking is inadequate for the courtroom.

For many years, my exercise consisted of jogging one day and going to the gym and lifting weights on machines on the alternate day. Neither required my mind to be engaged. I began to experiment with exercises and programs that required my mind to be aware of technique as well as breathing and form, such as the Five Tibetan Movements,[15] yoga-like exercises that require you to move slowly and concentrate on breathing and doing each exercise in the proper form. I gave up the weight room and learned the many techniques of kettlebells, in which the main goal is quality of form and body alignment and coordination of breathing with strength moves, rather than lifting the heaviest poundage.

I found that as I began to put my mind completely into my movements, my thinking was more relaxed and clearer afterward. The more I cleared my mind and thought about nothing other than the perfect form of the physical action and the coordination of breath, the more my physical being helped my concentration, my fluid thinking, and my cross-examination.

Breath

Body awareness begins with the breath. Rapid breathing is a subconscious reaction to stress activated by the sympathetic nervous system—the "fight or flight" response. In contrast, deliberate slow, deep breathing ac-

---

[15] Peter Kelder, *Ancient Secret of the Fountain of Youth* (New York: Doubleday, 1998).

tivates the relaxation response associated with the para-sympathetic nervous system, described by Harvard Medical School doctor Herbert Benson after studying it in transcendental meditators.[16] Yoga and martial arts prac-titioners have long known how to calm the body and mind through slow, deep breaths, a strategy also used by public speakers to reduce stage fright and anxiety.

Mindful breathing has direct importance for cross-examination. The tension that is the hallmark of the courtroom can take over the body and mind, creating a rigid and impermeable state that blocks clear per-ception and understanding of what is happening and reacting optimally to it. Proper breathing can release this tense and blocked state, putting you into that calm, focused flow state in which your intuition and memory can activate, in which the right question easily arises at the right time during cross-examination.

Mindful breathing, integrated into your life and legal practice, allows you to have better control over your body, your thoughts, and your emotions. It gives you the presence, charisma, and control that lead to the seamless, relaxed performance that is the mark of the master. It enhances your focus and perception, making you a better listener and giving you better mental clarity about what is happening in the courtroom. It helps you control the pace of your delivery so you don't rush, and to control the emotional tone of your cross-exami-nation. You can better exercise your instincts and access all the facts that you've studied without freezing up.

Mindful, slow breathing is a habit, just as tense, shallow breathing is a habit that many people are un-aware of. Your goal is to achieve a habitual relaxed state that you return to even under stress. This starts outside

---

[16] Herbert Benson, *The Relaxation Response* (New York: Harper Collins, 1975/2001).

the courtroom through both awareness of your breathing throughout the day and specific practices involving breath awareness, like meditation, yoga, and martial arts.

Posture

Along with breath, your posture both conveys credibility and promotes better thinking, listening, and speaking. Trials involve long periods of sitting. I tended to get uncomfortable and fatigued and then would lean forward with my arms on the table or slump back in my chair. After some experimentation, I found that sitting up with my back straight and unsupported made me less fatigued and more alert. It was hard at first so I began to focus on my posture, especially my lower back strength and flexibility, when I exercised. Spending time doing exercises that worked my back and posture (rather than simply trying to burn calories on a treadmill like a gerbil) also improved my standing posture and made it possible for me to stand straight with shoulders back and body and mind fluid and relaxed for longer periods of time. You will also find that if you sit and stand up straight you will immediately feel more energized, confident, and in control.

Prepare to think in flow

There are three interconnected fluid thinking skills: quick reasoning, abstract thinking, and improvising from knowledge. You can prepare in advance for the last two. Preparation can enhance quick reasoning, which is the tip of the spear in confronting a new problem. Almost every "new" problem will fall into a category of problems you have confronted before. You could relate every new problem conceptually to a previous problem. This is especially true in trial work. It has happened before, or something like it has happened before. So to prepare for abstract thinking you select the most likely ways to abstract or conceptualize what is happening.

By thinking in advance about abstract forms you do two things: (1) you can more quickly identify the abstract elements of the problem you're dealing with and (2) you can prepackage a finite number of potential actions (no more than three) to deal with the problem. This will increase your reasoning speed in real time because you will be ready with the weapons and actions to take at hand. For example, you can categorize witnesses as evasive, talkative, strident, and so on, connecting those qualities with counterstrategies that you've used successfully in the past and that we discussed in chapter 7.

In the same way you can prepare to improvise from your knowledge of facts and methods by figuring out what knowledge (the big facts) will most likely govern the situation, because the problem (the witness) is either confronting a big fact or avoiding one.

Using Fluid Thinking and the Mind-Body Connection in the Courtroom

The typical law school program teaches that being a lawyer is a mental profession that revolves around linear analytical and critical thinking. If you've been trained in that style, it can be hard to see the relevance of a shift to thinking of the law profession as a mind-body practice and of cross-examination, in particular, as best performed with intuitive fluid thinking. Can all this mind-body stuff actually make you a better courtroom lawyer? The answer is yes. Below are some suggestions for how you can use the mind-body connection and fluid thinking in the courtroom.

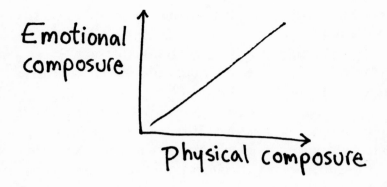

Control the courtroom by controlling yourself

Control of the courtroom begins with control of yourself. The courtroom can be a place of high drama and emotions. A lot is at stake for all parties. Moreover, lawyers feel like they're on stage and being judged on the quality of their performance by everyone in the courtroom. Having to manage large quantities of documents and information, be aware of everything that's happening, make rapid decisions, and ask the right questions can be highly stressful. You can only be successful at this if you control your emotions so that they help rather than hinder you.

If you learn to control first your breathing and then your whole body, you will be able to control your emotions. If you can control your emotions you can project this control to the entire room as calm confidence. The judge and jury will instinctively trust your character and what you're saying—Aristotle's ethos. Although you can't precisely control how they feel, you have quite a bit of power to influence their emotions, consistent with Aristotle's second mode of persuasion for public speaking, pathos. The words that you use instinctively when you're in a relaxed, self-controlled state will be more effective—more focused, more engaged and engaging, and on point.

Self-control also means being in control of your process of listening, perceiving, and estimating what could happen next based on what you perceive. This requires confidence that you will be able to deal with what happens next. It means that in your preparation you have thought through and rehearsed worst-case scenarios and are comfortable dealing with the worst-case answers to your questions. All of these benefits flow directly from the physical mode of thinking and the consciousness and mindfulness of your physical presence.

Finally, self-control means eliminating involuntary reactions to stress that undermine your presentation. When I was a young lawyer I thought that the best way to control the courtroom was to map out all of my questions and the witnesses' answers. I wrote out the answers that I wanted and expected to receive, and on paper all my cross-examinations ended brilliantly. But to my surprise, nobody was giving the answers I wrote out. So next I started writing out all possible answers I could think of, not just the ideal answer. If he says this, I'll ask that. That didn't work either. It was exhausting and I only grew more confused. In the courtroom I reacted to my frustration by getting mad. So mad that I got red in the face. Often I had to sit down to avoid looking like an overheated tomato. In a tense courtroom lawyers are subject to all kinds of tics and mannerisms, verbal and otherwise. It is common for lawyers to inject "Okay" before every question, button and unbutton a jacket, or repeatedly clear their throat without realizing they're doing it. These behaviors are generated by nerves and lack of presence and are seen by judges and juries, who use them to make negative judgments of your credibility and character.

At first I thought there was no way to control my red face, since it was an involuntary reaction. But when

I learned to practice breathing and body awareness, I was better able to deal with my frustration in the courtroom. I was able to remain calm and unflustered both physically and mentally when things didn't go according to the script. Involuntary reactions take up mental and physical energy and they distract you from the task at hand. Eliminate them through awareness of your mind and body and you will find you have better focus and stamina.

Abandon static plans, expect the unexpected, adapt to change

Because fluid intelligence evolved to solve problems in unstable situations, in order to tap into it you can't expect to simply follow your prepared checklist—"The witness will be evasive, therefore I will do A, B, and C." No. You must be prepared for what you are not prepared for.

Learning about and practicing fluid thinking convinced me that the script that I thought was my main cross-examination tool was part of the problem. There really can't be a script in a cross-examination. You have a set of facts and an end goal, but how you get there is constantly in flux. To stay a step ahead of the process you need to be in a fluid physical and mental state that allows you to respond flexibly to each event. If you write out a script during your preparation you will have a false sense of security that will only reassure you during your preparation. It will not hold up in the courtroom and it will leave you panicked as you flounder in your own excess of written questions and plans that aren't working.

But without a written script, how can you keep track of the hundreds, perhaps thousands of facts that make up your case? If you have prepared as described in chapter 4, the information you need is in your mind.

All the facts are there and interconnected logically because during your preparation you have made those connections. You have to enter into a fluid mind-body state so you can access them to move your cross-examination in the direction you want and solve any problems that arise. You have to trust that the process will work for you because you've prepared your case properly and you've practiced mind-body awareness on a daily basis. Instead of a script, have a number of goals, points, and topics written down in case you forget something.

Now that I'm no longer rigidly attached to a preset script, I can just ask questions and listen and react to what is actually happening. My questions are much better because they flow from the real events of the courtroom. I go into cross-examinations with a general map of the territory, goals, and facts, an inexact pre-science of what is going to happen, understanding it in terms of larger movements, but not even trying to think in terms of exactly what will happen. This allows me to be present, to experience the trial in the moment rather than to be burdened with trying to work out everything in advance and getting anxious when things don't go according to plan.

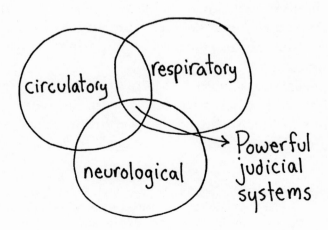

Conclusion

Concentrating on the body's physical processes promotes the kind of natural, fluid problem solving that the brain has evolved to do. A study conducted at Ludvich Maximillius University in Munich found that participants who had an awareness of and concentration on their heartbeat—those with good cardiac perception—consistently performed better at a gambling game that required quick, complex decision making compared to those with poor cardiac perception.[17] Of course thinking about your heartbeat all the time could be distracting when you cross-examine, but the point is that if you spend time becoming aware of your respiration, heartbeat, breath, and posture, you will improve your fluid thinking.

As the questioner you have the natural advantage of control. It is fluid thinking that generates the best next question. In the courtroom, the greatest thrill of cross-examination, the greatest rush of endorphins, dopamine, and other evolutionary brain chemicals happens when the witness makes some important but unexpected statement, and you quickly respond with a question, right on point, that puts the unexpected statement in alignment not with the witness's story strategy but with your own. When witnesses try to surprise you, you quickly respond by asking the very best next question.

This is the situation where the truth comes out, and that trials often turn on. It happens when you're thinking in just the way that evolution has designed the human brain to think at its best. It is drama, logic,

---

[17] Natalie S. Werner, Katharina Jung, Stefan Duschek, and Rainer Schandry, "Enhanced Cardiac Perception Is Associated with Benefits in Decision-Making," *Physiology* 46, no. 6 (2009, January): 1123–1129.

problem solving, truth finding, and fluid thinking all in one. These questions come when the whole person, body and mind, is engaged in the questioning process, when you enter the flow state described by psychologist Csikszentmihalyi. Since most lawyers are unaware of the importance of this type of thinking and the mind-body connection, you will have the upper hand if you integrate mind-body practices into your daily life and your practice as a lawyer.

CHAPTER SUMMARY

Main Takeaway

Cross-examination is a mind-body activity. The mind and body are inseparable and both need to be in excellent working order for optimal performance in the unpredictable environment of the courtroom. Cultivate mind and body in your daily life. Bring that presence into the courtroom.

Earthquake Points

- A physical presence in the courtroom will help you think better, get to the truth better, and persuade better.

- Presence and mindfulness send signals about your skill, confidence, intelligence, and sincerity to the judge and jury, which they equate with your credibility.

- Breathing is the connection between mind and body. When in doubt, breathe!

- Fluid thinking is a mind-body state that engages the whole person and helps you to quickly understand and respond to constantly changing events in the courtroom.

- Learn about and seek flow. This is the optimal physical and mental state for the cross-examiner.

- To think fluidly in the courtroom, integrate mind-body practices into your personal and working life.

- Practice good physical care with attention to breath, exercise, sleep, nutrition, and stress reduction.

- Expect the unexpected and adapt to changes. Don't become rigidly attached to your plans and scripts. If you have prepared deeply your instinct and intuition will allow you to flow with events in the courtroom.

CHAPTER 10

LEARNING AND MASTERY

Learn → Practice } Never
       ↓   stop
     — Improve }

I N THIS BOOK I HAVE PROPOSED some concepts that
are off the beaten path for most lawyers because they
aren't drawn specifically from the set of legal and analytical skills that most lawyers think of as good lawyering. Trials and cross-examination are an afterthought
in most law-school programs. Legal academies don't
seem to take cross-examination seriously as a field
worthy of study. Another important omission in law
schools is attention to lifelong learning as an important
field of study in itself. The "truth" in the Truth Engine is
neither black and white nor static. You must constantly
seek it, pursue it, learn it. Thus learning is an essential
part of the Truth Engine. This chapter will explore what
it means to truly master cross-examination and how to
approach learning higher levels of cross-examination
skills. Your traditionally trained adversary may not be
aware of the array of methods described here, giving you
the competitive edge if you're willing to devote time to

understanding what mastery is and to practice it.

In this chapter we will be learning about learning. It is important to think of learning not as something separate but as an integral part of the process of cross-examination. It is often beneficial to step out of law completely when preparing to cross-examine or preparing a trial and to spend some time thinking about learning itself.

I have stressed in previous chapters that trials and cross-examination never stand still, they are constantly evolving. I have also said that cross-examination involves all aspects of the lawyer as a person: the mind, the body, the emotional self, character, the moral and ethical self, the intuitive self. These aspects of the self are also (ideally) constantly developing over the course of your lifetime as you mature as a person. And of course the field of law and the types of cases that lawyers handle are continually changing and becoming more complex. These constant changes mean that we must always be adapting and learning, and so the subject of learning itself is important for lawyers to study.

Cross-examination is worthy of devoted lifelong learning and practice because it has a great impact on people's lives and fortunes. If musicians, athletes, and other high-level competitors spend their whole working lives practicing and learning, then surely lawyers should be engaged in this as well, given the importance of what we do. More is on the line in the most mundane trial—an eviction or foreclosure case, for example—than in a virtuoso piano performance, and some lawsuits impact millions of people.

By "learning" I mean not just learning the law or learning the facts of a case, but learning about the process by which knowledge and skills improve. Just as previous chapters contrasted a broader and deeper way of thinking about cross-examination with conventional law-school methods of thinking, so also in this chapter, the learning style I recommend for mastery of cross-examination is not the way that you learn in law school. In fact this kind of learning is not the kind of learning that I was taught. I used to associate learning with studying, mnemonics of the kind I used to study for the bar exam, and other memory techniques. These things are useful to trial lawyers. But this kind of learning is best applied to static situations, such as test taking and giving a set speech, where you're not confronted with an opposing force face-to-face. The approach to learning that I advocate here is much better suited to the fluid, constantly changing conditions of adversarial trials and cross-examination.

In previous chapters we have addressed the individual elements of cross-examination: seeking the truth, perceiving facts, immersive preparation, telling a story, strategy, fluid thinking, physical presence, and so on. Mastery of cross-examination means continually learning and consciously practicing each of these elements one by one and then bringing them all together in unison at a continuously higher level, so that these skills are available to you intuitively at the critical moment. This is what I refer to as the "spiral of mastery." Ultimately, the lawyer who understands the forces at work beneath a successful courtroom performance and can pull them all together instinctively as a result of daily internalized practice inside and outside the courtroom will have the advantage over the lawyer who merely excels at the law.

What Is a Master Cross-Examiner?

A master cross-examiner is one who knows the facts of the case and can ask the right question in any situation. "Right question" means one that finds the truth, tells the story, and advances your strategy. A right question is formed in brief and powerful words and spoken in a way that persuades. "Any situation" means planned or unplanned, set up or spontaneous.

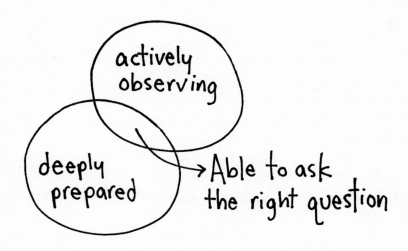

In this book we have seen that cross-examination involves all aspects of the lawyer: your practical knowledge, your understanding of a broad range of interconnected skills, your intuitive sense of human nature, your emotional and physical presence in the courtroom. It is not enough to be a master of either practical knowledge or of these other nontraditional skills. Both are necessary. These two different approaches to cross-examination are exemplified by the lists of skills and qualities of the master lawyer put forth by two master cross-examiners: Irving Younger and Peter Megargee Brown.

Irving Younger's Ten Commandments of Cross Examination, listed in chapter 1, are essential technical rules that must be mastered by every cross-examiner: be brief, use plain words, use only leading questions, and so on. But they don't speak to the many other factors that enter into a masterful cross-examination. They are valuable, but they are discrete skills unconnected to any underlying principles. Lawyer Peter Megargee Brown (1922–2014), like Younger an assistant U.S. Attorney for the Southern District of New York, long-time private practitioner, and author, proposed a list of ten qualities of a master cross-examiner:[1]

1. A thorough understanding of human nature

2. Clear, logical thinking and presentation

3. Communicating in direct, simple, coherent thoughts

4. Judgment or a sense of proportion in evaluating and reacting to everything that occurs during the trial

5. Self-discipline

6. Conveying an impression of authority

7. A dignified and courteous manner

8. A personality that allows you to influence those around you

9. Compulsiveness for thorough preparation

10. The absence of trickery and subterfuge

What is most striking about Brown's qualities is that only one of them refers specifically to the practice of law. They are far more behavior and character based than Younger's technical rules. They are actually remi-

---

[1] Paraphrased from Peter Megargee Brown, *The Art of Questioning: Thirty Maxims of Cross-Examination* (New York: Macmillan, 1987), xviii.

niscent of classical Greek descriptions of what makes a "fine and good" person. They can apply to any area of endeavor, not just cross-examination and not just law.

Our definition of mastery is not yet complete. A third marker of the master cross-examiner is mastery of the body, mind, and spirit simultaneously. George Leonard (1923–2010), a writer and educator associated with the Esalen Institute, wrote extensively about education and human potential. He earned a black belt in aikido and from aikido principles he developed Leonard Energy Training (LET), which uses the physical body to increase mental and spiritual awareness. In his book *Mastery: The Keys to Success and Longterm Fulfillment* he emphasizes that mastery means lifelong devotion to your craft and integration of mind, body, and spirit. Mastery is a journey marked by spurts and plateaus of progress, Leonard says: "This journey will take you along a path that is both arduous and exhilarating. It will bring you unexpected heartaches and unexpected rewards, and you will never reach a final destination. . . . You'll probably end up learning as much about yourself as about the skill you're pursuing."[2]

For a lawyer and cross-examiner, mastery means setting yourself on the path of years-long practice, beginning with Younger's ten commandments, striving to exemplify Brown's character traits, and integration of mind, body, and spirit as taught by Leonard. All of this happens in your office during preparation, in the courtroom, and in your daily life beyond the courtroom. If you approach learning to become a master in this comprehensive, holistic way, you will have many advantages and insights that other lawyers lack as they focus mainly on the technical aspects of the profession. There

---

[2] George Leonard, *Mastery: The Keys to Success and Longterm Fulfillment* (New York: Penguin, 1992), 14.

may be long plateaus, frustrating because there is no visible progress, but you will develop the qualities of an excellent lawyer, thinker, and human being. You will gradually, almost imperceptibly, grow into mastery.

The Connection between Learning and Mastery

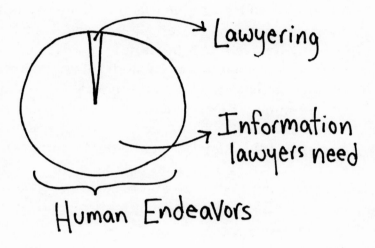

Cross-examination is not an arcane, isolated activity practiced only by clever lawyers with esoteric knowledge. It is a fundamental form of human thinking and being that supports the demands of high-level performance and competition. In trials the full gamut of human experience plays out in conflicts that cannot be framed only in legal terms or resolved only with technical legal skill. We can learn much about the nature of these conflicts and how to solve them (meaning win them) by studying other fields of human thought, experience, and endeavor: philosophy, the arts (film, theatre, and literature), psychology, neuropsychology, warfare, games, martial arts, and biology, for example.

243

Many high-performance disciplines require alternating between study, contemplation, and practice in a continual spiral of learning, leading ultimately to mastery. The spiral of learning and mastery is well known to great performers like musicians, martial artists, athletes, and actors. Although they devote thousands of hours of practice to attaining mastery, their mastery arises from much more than technical skill in their fields. A devotion to learning marks the master in most fields. Lawyers perform under similar conditions of pressure and we have much to learn by studying how other masters learn their crafts. I will draw on the ideas of two grand masters—in chess and martial arts—who have devoted much of their attention to the process of learning and mastery to help you understand several underlying principles that connect being, learning, and mastery—principles that go well beyond mere technical skill. Cross-examination as an art has more in common with these other fields than with the interpretation of statutes and cases.

The Unity between Life and Competitive Performance

American chess master and martial arts champion Joshua Waitzkin (born 1976) has devoted a large part of his career to understanding learning and mastery. A child prodigy, by age ten he was competing against adult masters, including Garry Kasparov; at sixteen he was an International Master; and by eighteen he had won the U.S. Junior Chess championship twice. The movie *Searching for Bobby Fischer* chronicles his childhood. In part to escape the pressures of his fame, he learned tai chi and jiujitsu in his twenties and became a world champion performer and coach.

Waitzkin's book *The Art of Learning: An Inner Journey to Optimal Performance* discusses a type of learning that can be optimally applied to cross-examination. The book describes Waitzkin's journey from chess master to what appears on the surface to be an entirely different field of learning, tai chi. One of his essential discoveries was that the two fields of study—and intuitively many other competitive endeavors that demand a high level of mind/body skill—are "linked by an essential connecting ground."[3]

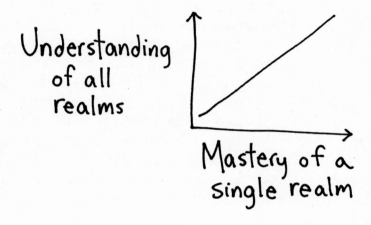

As he moved from the ostensibly cerebral discipline of chess to the highly physical martial arts, he felt the unity in all his actions. He found himself using chess principles in tai chi and tai chi flow in chess. The dissolution of barriers between the two became an end in itself. That is, he became better at both skills by focusing on the art of learning as a unifying ground. He studied philosophy and found an underlying unity in various Eastern and Western principles, which he described as "the study of numbers to leave numbers or form to

---

[3] Josh Waitzkin, *The Art of Learning: An Inner Journey to Optimal Performance* (New York: Free Press, 2007), xiv.

leave form."[4] By leaving the discipline and turning your attention to the way your body and mind take it in, you actually reach it at a deeper level. I am using the words "higher" and "deeper" to mean the same thing, even though in a physical sense that would be contradictory. The spiral of mastery goes either to higher or deeper levels of understanding. If you look deeply enough into chess, numbers, or the facts of a case, you understand the thing you are studying at a higher level, but you also gain life wisdom and insight into human nature.

An important part of Waitzkin's teaching is setting aside a single-minded focus on winning and shifting your focus to higher principles and goals. He writes, "The game had become endlessly fascinating to me and its implications stretched far beyond winning and losing. I was no longer primarily refining the skill of playing chess, but was discovering myself through chess."[5] For the lawyer this means adopting a learning mindset: you are learning the truth of your case, learning how to best unveil that truth in cross-examination, and learning about yourself and the human experience at an ever-higher level.

The Spiral of Mastery: Mastery of the Basics

The spiral of mastery is made up of the fundamentals covered in this book, continually developed and combined: Irving Younger's Ten Commandments of Cross Examination, the nature of facts, of human memory and perception, the elements of story, principles of strategy, and so on. To initiate the spiral of mastery you start at the bottom with a single element. You

---

[4] Ibid., 95.
[5] Ibid., 70.

set everything else aside and simply focus on learning what a fact is and what part of the information you have in your case is really facts. Then you think about whether these facts suggest a story, and to do that, you focus on what a story is—what are the elements of a story and how do they work together? You will find that when you have thought about facts as they relate to a story, you understand facts at a higher level than when you thought about them alone. When you think about preparation and immersion you will join new and better insights to your facts and story. When you move to thinking about how to present your story strategically you will gain ever more insights and discoveries about facts, about story, about how to prepare. When you practice physically as described earlier in this book you move up to yet another level, and when you think about the process of learning, you gain still more. Then, when you return to the simple facts you started with, you understand them better, having wound up the spiral and returned, but at a higher level.

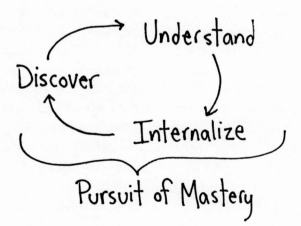

As you learn more about these fundamentals you internalize them and they become interconnected subconsciously. Eventually, as Waitzkin writes, the process "continuously cycles along as deeper layers of the art are soaked in."[6]

Learning Flow

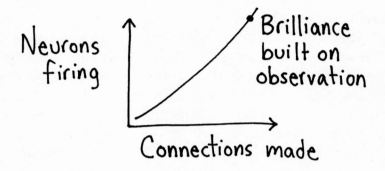

The spiral of mastery also applies to learning optimal mind-body states. In chapter 9 we saw how important the flow state of being deeply absorbed in the present moment is to cross-examination. As an intense competitor, Josh Waitzkin uses this flow state, which he calls the "soft zone," to avoid emotional reactions to mistakes, which can cause cascading errors that often undo even high-level competitors. He describes a moment in a chess match when he was deeply absorbed in trying to figure out a difficult situation. Suddenly an earthquake shook the building, but it did not interrupt his focus. "I was aware of myself and the shaking world from within the serenity of pure engagement," he writes.[7] As the earth shook, the solution to his dilemma arose from his

[6] Ibid., xvii.
[7] Ibid., 55.

subconscious. Learning to be in this soft zone underlies Waitzkin's approach to both chess and martial arts: "My understanding of learning was about searching for the flow that lay at the heart of and transcended the technical," he says.[8]

Searching for this state is time well spent during your preparation for a case. When I first began cross-examination, I was fascinated by the feeling I had when I put aside the winning or losing of my case and concentrated on the technique of cross-examination. My mind was completely open to learning because I had little experience to fall back on. I said to myself, win or lose, I'm going to do this the right way. During my preparation I focused on short, simple, one-fact questions. I felt myself relaxing and everything began to flow. In the courtroom I lost my self-consciousness and nervousness and was able to simply focus and react, often very well.

Flow is about connections, about approaching cross-examination holistically to unite the perceptive, the logical, the intuitive, the physical, the psychological. It's important to learn this flow state during your preparation so that you come to rely on your internal resources rather than being buffeted by external events. But like all skills, the flow state comes gradually as you ascend the spiral of mastery.

Leonard's Master Keys Applied to Cross-Examination

In his book *Mastery*, George Leonard has five short chapters on the five "master keys," which are Instruction, Practice, Surrender, Intentionality, and the Edge.[9]

---

[8] Ibid., 95.
[9] Leonard, *Mastery*, 53–101.

Each of these keys has a direct application to cross-examination and can contribute to the holistic approach to mastery that lawyers should seek.

1. Instruction and feedback

In contrast to the usual method of learning alone, learners of cross-examination should look to a teacher or mentor to practice with and accept criticism from. Cross-examination and trials are fraught with stress and ego. When I was a young lawyer any criticism was painful, especially when I was told I was doing it wrong. For lawyers, one's mentor is usually one's boss, making criticism even harder to take. But Olympic athletes have coaches who know them, prepare them, work together with them, and advise them during contests. Why not have a coach for cross-examination? Try to find one who will work with you at every stage, focusing on the craft before the result, maybe someone outside your legal chain of command.

2. Practice

Trial lawyers differ from other high-pressure performers in one important respect. While athletes, musicians, and chess players are often completely absorbed day and night in relentless practice and study, cross-examiners derive much of their understanding of their craft from living in and studying the real world. There are some trial lawyers who live and die law, trials, and work, but they are not always the best. The best trial lawyers live a balanced life of awareness of the goings-on of the real world and the humans in it.

Opportunities for practice of legal skills abound in daily life. You can seek a relaxed state of flow when you're exercising, playing music, playing sports or games, or singing. Because the important elements of cross-examination are not confined to courtrooms or legal settings, you can visit and practice some part of cross-examination each day by looking at all legal and daily events through the lens of cross-examination. Every day you encounter facts, narratives, stories, and situations where you employ strategy. The kind of thinking used by a cross-examiner is not only useful in law, but in life. Insights about behavior, human nature, and character that are needed for cross-examination come from an observation of these in everyday life. And throughout each day you can become aware of your breathing, your posture, and your physical presence, connecting these to your thinking and speaking. This daily awareness and practice will build your intuition, consistency, and fluidity in the courtroom.

Rehearsal is an important practice strategy. You must learn doing by doing. A lawyer sitting, reviewing papers to prepare for cross-examination is no big deal. But getting someone to play a witness is a production. Try it for a limited, controlled session for an important witness and it will pay dividends for the whole case.

3. Be patient and accept risks and mistakes

If you're really learning, you're always making mistakes. This is what Leonard means when he talks about "surrender" and the "edge." The patience to endure your mistakes and still keep taking risks is an important force moving your learning forward. In cross-examination, more than with most skills, there are innumerable mistakes to be made. You must let go of your fear of mistakes. Surrender to it. This allows you to operate on the "edge," the risk zone where greater success is possible.

In chess there are thousands of books describing good moves to make and bad moves to avoid. For cross-examination there are perhaps a dozen books. There are plenty of uncharted mistakes to explore. You might make a mistake and a right move on the same question. For example, you might get the topic right but ask a sloppy question. You learn, you adjust, you patiently move closer to the right question on your next try.

4. Be aware, mindful, and intentional

In each case there is so much information to absorb that you can lose focus on improving your craft. But learning the craft will help you succeed as much as learning any case-specific information, in fact probably more. So if you stay aware of the elements of cross-examination we have discussed in this book and determine, with intent, to learn them as you work through the facts and stresses of each case, you will find yourself on the path to mastery.

Progress in your skill is not linear but happens below the surface, subconsciously. When learning becomes an end in itself, not drudgery, not preparing for something, you can make steady improvements without self-consciousness or inhibitions. You will find insights that help you win while losing the emotional burden of feeling yourself on display in the courtroom in a high-wire win-or-lose situation. In this mindset, you can take risks and feel more comfortable in the uncertain, like encountering a question on a test on material you haven't studied. You can learn your way through it. Adaptation and improvisation are aspects of fluid learning. Risk mistakes, embrace imperfection, find peace with it. If you're ready to suffer the indignities of mistakes and failure you will be in the best position to use imperfection, surprise, and disruption to your advantage.

Conclusion

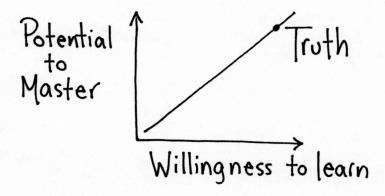

In chapter 1 I defined cross-examination as "asking questions that find and reveal the truth." It seems to me that learning has exactly the same definition. As you ask questions that reveal the truth, you learn. Learning is not just about absorbing information or preparing for a case. Learning is the act, the event, the game itself. A learner takes in information in order to discover new insights, truths, ways, paths, and methods.

For the lawyer there is a constant search for the connecting ground between technical skill, the whole person, and basic life principles. The face-to-face competitive nature of cross-examination makes it an activity closely associated with learning. In this kind of competition the choice is to learn or fail. You cannot rest on experience, expertise, or static knowledge. You will never finish learning how to cross-examine because each trial is a new learning experience. Learning is an integral part of cross-examination, and the type of holistic learning described by Waitzkin and Leonard, which they applied successfully to top levels of competition in chess and martial arts, is the only approach that fully meets the needs of the cross-examiner. Younger's Ten Commandments are very comforting to lawyers who like a clear and simple set of rules, but they're not enough for learning the full gamut of skills that come into play in the courtroom and make the difference between the technical expert and the master.

CHAPTER SUMMARY

Main Takeaway

A learning mind is integral to cross-examination. A focus on and awareness of the nature of learning will place you on the lifelong path of mastery.

Earthquake Points

- Mastery of cross-examination means continually practicing and uniting the essential elements of seeking the truth: perceiving facts, deep preparation, storytelling, strategy, fluid thinking, and learning itself.

- Learning takes place holistically during preparation, in the courtroom, and in your daily life.

- Cross-examination is like other high-performance arts that involve study, contemplation, and practice to achieve mastery, like music, chess, the martial arts, and athletics. Observe how the masters in those fields constantly learn and perfect their craft.

- A learning mindset means learning the truth of your case, learning how to unveil that truth, and learning about yourself and the human experience at an ever-higher level.

- An important benefit of the learning mindset is the flow state that goes beyond technical expertise to unite perceptions, logic, intuition, mind, and body.

- The spiral of mastery begins with mastery of the basics. As you return to the basics with each new case or problem, you will understand them at a higher level. With a deeper understanding, this continual return at a higher level is the spiral of mastery.